7022

A
HOUSE FULL
of Friends

To Phyllis
Blessings!

Susan Yates

Other Books by Susan Alexander Yates:

*And Then I Had Kids: Encouragement for Mothers of
Young Children*
Word Publishing
Dallas, Texas
©1988

*What Really Matters at Home: Eight Crucial Elements for
Building Character in Your Family*
John and Susan Yates
Word Publishing
Dallas, Texas
©1992

A HOUSE FULL of Friends

How to Like
the Ones You Love

Susan Alexander Yates

PUBLISHING
Colorado Springs, Colorado

A HOUSE FULL OF FRIENDS

Library of Congress Cataloging-in-Publication Data
Yates, Susan Alexander.
    House full of friends: How to like the ones you love / by Susan Yates.
        p. cm.
    ISBN 1-56179-343-4
    1. Family.   2. Interpersonal relations.   I. Title.
HQ518.Y37   1995
306.87—dc20   94-38884
                                                                                CIP

Published by Focus on the Family Publishing,
Colorado Springs, Colorado 80995.
Distributed by Word Books, Dallas, Texas.

Unless otherwise noted, Scripture quotations are from the HOLY BIBLE, NEW INTER-
NATIONAL VERSION, ©1973, 1978, 1984 by the International Bible Society. Used by
permission of Zondervan Publishing House. All rights reserved. Quotations identified as
NASB are from the New American Standard Bible, ©1960, 1963, 1968, 1971, 1973,
1975, and 1977 by The Lockman Foundation. Used by permission.

Editor: Gwen Weising
Designer: B.C. Studios
Photographer for Yates Family: Kathryn Zerbian

Printed in the United States of America

95 96 97 98 99/10 9 8 7 6 5 4 3 2 1

To my sister,
Fran Alexander Cade,
and my brothers,
Frank Alexander and Syd Alexander, Jr.

With thanksgiving for your
inspiration, encouragement, love,
and friendships

Contents

Acknowledgments

PART ONE: **My Family, My Friends**

1. A Family Storybook 3
2. A Vision for Your Family 11

PART TWO: **What Does It Take to Make a Family of Friends?**

3. Security: The Foundation for Family Friendships 21
4. Encouragement: The Helping Hand for
   Family Friendships 31
5. Respect: The Place of Honor in Family Friendships 41
6. Celebration: The Daily Joy of Family Friendships 49
7. Prayer: The Invisible Bond of Family Friendships 61

PART THREE: **Cultivating Our Closest Friendships**

8. Friendship Between Husband and Wife............................73
9. Friendships Between Parents and Young Children 85
10. Friendships Between Siblings 95
11. Friendships Between Parents and Teenagers 109
12. Friendships Between Parents and Adult Children 125

PART FOUR: **Forging Bonds Between Generations**

13. Strengthening Friendships with Parents and In-Laws 137
14. Forging Bonds Between Grandparents and
    Grandchildren 151
15. Caring for the Extended Family 163
16. Friendships in Single-Parent and Blended Families 173

EPILOGUE:
Yours Can Be a Family of Friends 185

Notes 189

Acknowledgments

Writing a book on family friendships has reminded me how grateful I am for many people. My best friend, my husband, John, encourages me and makes our marriage a treasure. Our children, Libby, Susy, Chris, John, and Allison, have been the greatest gifts in my life. They edit my work, let me tell stories about them, and keep me honest. My new son-in-law, Will Gaskins, is an answer to our prayers of 22 years for our daughter Allison. We feel so privileged that he has joined our family. My mom, Frances Alexander, and my mother-in-law, Sue Yates, have been wonderful role models for me and have prayed for me daily.

In my larger "family," four women in my covenant group pray faithfully for me and hold me accountable. I'm grateful for Anne Cregger, Jane Eboch, Kim Doerr, and Tucker Viccellio. Good friends Holly Leachman, Ann Holladay, Ann Hibbard, Beth Spring, Brenda Hunter, Elaine Metcalf, Betsy Roadman, and Heidi Metcalf have encouraged me and given me feedback along the way. I'm also grateful to Elizabeth Brunner and Jeff Taylor for their valuable professional comments.

Those at Focus on the Family have truly become a family. I'm thankful for Al Janssen and his hard-working team. My editor, Gwen Weising, has wise insights and is a delight to work with. She possesses a spirit of joy and a great laugh that makes work fun. My agent, Stephen Griffith, graciously handles publishing details for me.

The "family" members at The Falls Church, an Episcopal church where my husband is the rector, have been an encouragement for nearly 16 years. Many of them have generously shared their stories in this book. They have surrounded our family with love, picking us up when we fall, cheering us on when we are tired, encouraging us to keep growing in family friendships, and inspiring us to trust Christ daily.

And finally, my sister, Fran, and my brothers, Syd and Frank. You have been there from the beginning and you have taught me what a treasure family friendships are. It's to you that I dedicate this book with a grateful heart.

PART ONE

My Family, My Friends

CHAPTER 1

A Family Storybook

Ah, Lord God!
Behold, Thou hast made the heavens and the earth
by Thy great power
and by Thine outstretched arm!
Nothing is too difficult for Thee.

Jeremiah 32:17 *(NASB)*

I was sitting at a picnic table with two sisters in their late teens. For nearly a week I had watched them with each other. A shared hug of friendly companionship; a joke whispered between them followed by roars of laughter; a quiet act of thoughtfulness as one did a task for the other; a moment of bragging about each other to a group of friends; and a genuine sense of pure joy as they worked side by side.

These girls truly love each other, I thought. *It's natural, and it seems to pull those around them into a circle of love and kindness. This is the kind of relationship I want my children to have with each other. I wonder what kind of family these girls come from? How did their parents raise children like this?*

John and I and our children were on a small island off the coast of

British Columbia participating in a family conference. Nearly everyone there was sleeping in tents and eating food prepared from a small trailer.

Elna was one of the two sisters. She was the chief cook for the summer. Her sister Heidi had come to help for a week. After watching them for several days, I knew I had to talk to them. I had to know about their background, and I wanted to learn about their family's friendships.

"Tell me about your family," I suggested when we sat together after breakfast one morning. As I listened and asked questions, I began to catch a glimpse of a family whose members were genuine friends with one another and I began to learn why.

Elna and Heidi were two of 11 children born to a couple who had immigrated to Canada from The Netherlands. They had grown up on a small farm.

"Mom and Dad always had clear family policies," one said. "Breakfast was a family affair, and we were all expected to be there. At dinnertime Dad would read the Scriptures to us while we took turns cleaning up. We all had chores, so we grew up learning the value of hard work. Doing chores together also helped us build a sense of teamwork.

"Mom and Dad were great with fun and games. Saturday nights were family fun nights. We built forts in the barn and had races around the house. Often we pulled out special board games reserved for family nights. Mom and Dad always joined in the games. Mom taught us how to cut pictures out of Sears catalogs to make paper dolls and paper houses."

"What was your parents' relationship like?" I asked.

"Mom and Dad have always been a team," Elna replied. "They've always supported each other. If we tried to get around one of them by going to the other, the response was usually, 'Wait until your mother (or father) and I discuss it.'

"Dad always courted Mom. Each spring when the first flowers bloomed, he picked a bunch and marched up the driveway hiding the bouquet behind his back. With a gleam in his eyes, he rang the front doorbell and presented them to Mom. She always made a big fuss over him. He did the same thing with the first blackberries. He always wanted Mom to have his 'firsts.'"

As these girls spoke with fondness about their parents and siblings, I thought, *What an amazing family! I wish I could spend time with all of them.*

Their family relationships seemed almost unbelievable—a throwback to another century—but this was today, and they seemed to really enjoy one another. Against tremendous odds, including a tight budget and great cultural barriers, they had cultivated a family whose members genuinely loved and took pride in one another.

As I listened to them, I thought, *Isn't this what we all want? A family with this kind of loving loyalty toward one another?*

But what if my family isn't like this? you may ask. *What if I am a single parent?*

My friend Jana was in this position. She had been married for just five years when she and her husband divorced. Their two-year-old son, Bruce, continued to live with his mother. In the beginning, Jana did not communicate well with her ex-husband. They argued over finances and visitation plans. Every conversation was a potential eruption. Long hours of work left her exhausted; a tight budget limited new toys and special outings for Bruce; Jana was having a tough time raising him alone.

Long before the divorce, Jana had stopped going to church. However, she now felt that she needed to find a church home for herself and her young son. A friend invited her to a church where she found love, support, and most important of all, a vital faith. But she continued to struggle in her family relationships. Several couples reached out and invited her to join them in a study about cultivating healthy families. She and her son spent time with these couples and their children. They laughed together, cried together, and grew to love one another and each other's children.

Jana and Bruce's friendship deepened as she learned to let her errands wait and spend time with him. They cultivated their common interest in history by going to museums together and by reading the same books.

As she grew in her faith, Jana realized that she needed to take steps toward improving her relationship with Bruce's dad. She wanted their relationship to be pleasant for the sake of their son, yet she knew that she had made many mistakes both in her marriage and afterward. So she wrote her ex-husband to tell him that she accepted responsibility for what she had contributed to the breakup of their marriage. She asked his forgiveness. She learned to say "I'm sorry" when she was rude to him, and she encouraged Bruce's friendship with his dad.

Gradually, over many years, her relationship with Bruce's dad has gone from being an angry, conflict-filled association to a cooperative, amicable relationship. Her friendship with her son has also grown. It was a highlight when Bruce, now a teenager, came to her and said, "Mom, when people ask me if I'm from a broken home, I tell them, 'My home is not broken. My parents are just divorced.'"

Even if you, like Jana, are a single parent . . . *It is still possible to cultivate a family marked by friendship.*

But what if our family circumstances are really difficult?

Lauren's most dominant feature is her huge smile. It spreads across her entire face, seeming to reach from ear to ear. Lauren is an unusual child. Born with a rare chromosomal abnormality, she has severe physical and mental retardation. At age 10, she cannot speak or care for herself in any way. Her younger sister, Emily, is five and is an unusually bright child. By the age of 18 months, Emily had already begun to speak in sentences.

Recently, I chatted with the girls' mom, Sharon, about the challenges of raising them.

"Susan," she reflected, "more than anything, I know we were chosen to be a family. God chose us to be parents to both Lauren and Emily. They have *both* enriched our lives and each other's lives."

Before Lauren was born, Sharon wasn't even sure she wanted children. She was on a fast track in her career and enjoying the material benefits of a generous salary. Hers was a world of intelligent, successful people. Then Lauren arrived and overnight her world changed.

It took Lauren's problems to show both Sharon and her husband, Edward, what was really important in life. It wasn't success; it was family and relationships. Caring for Lauren revealed a hidden side of Sharon. She became more sensitive and thrived in caring for this child, even though for years there was no response. She learned the meaning of unconditional love.

Sharon and Edward's marriage grew. They realized that small irritants in their relationship weren't worth getting upset over. Instead, God gave them additional grace to cope.

The girls have become dependent upon each other. Emily stimulates Lauren in play and helps dress her. From Lauren, Emily has learned sensitivity.

Recently, when the whole family was out, they noticed a boy in a wheelchair with severe cerebral palsy. Emily went right up to him and began to rub his arm and talk to him. As the grown-ups talked, she continued speaking to the boy. When it came time to leave, little Emily leaned over and kissed him on the cheek. Tears clouded his mother's eyes, but to Emily, it was simply the natural thing to do. Lauren had taught her well.

Loyalty, acceptance, and love characterize this family. They are mutually dependent upon one another, and they realize that each has something to teach the others. As Sharon remarked, "When difficulty comes, you must decide if it is going to be an expanding or contracting experience for you and your family."

Sharon and Edward have acquired a perspective that enables them to appreciate the unique personalities God uses to develop friendships within the family.

Even if we, like Sharon and Edward, face a difficult family situation . . .
We can still grow in friendship and love as a family.

But what if we come from a dysfunctional family?

Joe was the first of two boys. Because he was so athletic, he was the apple of his father's eye. His dad loved to roughhouse with him and he encouraged him to be tough. For Dad, aggression was the sign of manhood. Joe's younger brother was a very sensitive child with a slight build. He disliked sports and shunned physical activity. His tendency to recoil from aggressive play irritated his dad, and he began to make fun of this son. During playtimes, the father often encouraged the athletic brother to rough up the younger one. Soon, the younger boy became the object of sarcastic comments and subtle ridicule. The parents applauded the elder son's accomplishments while ignoring the younger son.

Gradually, the first brother grew to dislike his younger brother. After all, the younger brother didn't seem as "acceptable" as he was. Perhaps the parents did not realize the impact their attitude had on their sons. But today, the elder brother, Joe, now a parent himself, talks with sadness of the pain he caused his younger brother, who has adopted a gay life-style and who is filled with bitterness. Over the years, Joe has sought reconciliation and reached out to his brother with love, but there has been no response yet. So Joe continues to pray for him.

Fortunately, Joe's wife came from a loving, close-knit family. By watching her family interact and by talking with other healthy families, Joe learned ways to avoid the mistakes his parents made and to help his own children learn to honor and value one another. His desire is that with God's help and the encouragement of positive role models, his own family can be the first of a legacy of families whose members genuinely love one another.

Even if we, like Joe, have experienced abuse and pain in our families . . .

We can still be the first of a generation of healthy families, families whose members are friends with each other.

What if we're so overwhelmed with commitments in life that we're doing all we can just to make it through the day? How can we have time to cultivate family friendships?

Ogburn was a very successful executive, an entrepreneur with his own fast-growing business. He was a loving father of two small children with a third on the way. His marriage was good, and he and his wife were pillars of the local church. Because he was recognized as a leader in the community, many people sought his expertise. He was asked to serve on various boards and to consult with civic leaders. Whenever he could find spare time, he headed for the golf course. His wife supported him and understood his need for some time to himself. But she also realized that he was away from home a lot.

Ogburn was unusually close to his mother-in-law. For years she had told him how proud of him she was. She was interested in everything he did. Because his mother-in-law had a keen business sense, Ogburn often asked her advice on business matters. She also had unusual insight into people and gave Ogburn wise counsel in personnel matters. But more than anything, she loved him.

One day she asked Ogburn to go for a ride with her. "Ogburn," she began, "those little boys of yours are so precious. I know you don't get to spend much time with them. When they get bigger, they are going to want to talk with you about all sorts of things. If you don't make time to play with them *now*, when they are small, they won't talk to you when they are older. Why don't you find something that you can do with them?"

Ogburn listened to his mother-in-law, and the next day he gave his golf clubs away, piled his wife and two toddlers into the car, and said, "We're going out to look for a little farm to buy where we can have horses and be together on my day off."

For the next year, every Sunday after church the family packed a picnic and rode along the back roads of North Carolina in search of a small farm. Ogburn's Sunday afternoon golf game couldn't hold a candle to these picnics with his young family. In time, they found a small farm, bought it, and on his day off, Ogburn taught his boys, their new sister, and later, another son, to ride horseback. They watched cows give birth, got muddy, played in the hay, and threw horseshoes with their dad. They built a friendship that would impact generations to come.

A wise mother-in-law and a son-in-law who was willing to make hard choices for the good of his family made a difference in my life. That young business executive was my father-in-law.

Even if you feel overwhelmed with commitments . . . *Still, when we make tough choices, we take small steps in building family friendships.*

What if our attempts at family togetherness seem to backfire?

We had five children in seven years. Allison had just turned seven and our boys, John and Chris, were four and two, when we were surprised with twins, Susy and Libby! To say those early years were overwhelming would be a gross understatement. Most of the time, I felt like a walking zombie, simply trying to exist until somebody took a nap. I remember a child saying, "Ah, Mom, how come I have to take a nap when you're the one who's tired?"

Yet, even when the children were small, I wanted more than anything for them to be close, to love one another, and to have a close relationship with John and me. Both John and I were fortunate to come from strong, loving families, so we had the benefit of good role models. But I knew our heritage wasn't a guarantee that everything would work out well in our family. So I set out to read everything I could find about raising strong families. The books I read had many good points and several of them suggested that family camping was THE WAY to build a close-knit family.

You guessed it. I decided that if we were to be a family of friends, we had to go camping. So one year when spring vacation rolled around, we went to the camping store. We rented huge backpacks, tents, cooking utensils, and everything else we could conceivably need (and stuff we didn't) for a week-long "family-building" hike on the Appalachian trail.

I should have known we were in trouble when our five-year-old twins staggered under the weight of their backpacks after only 100 feet. Chris's and John's appreciation of nature was not enhanced by the blaring of their Walkmans. And while Allison pouted at leaving her teenage friends, my husband struggled to balance the Coleman stove and extra water bottles on his back. Undaunted, I exuded enthusiasm as our golden retriever, Duchess, raced ahead of us on the trail.

We hiked two miles the first day before we made camp and cooked our supper. No one was excited about my genuine camping food. Somehow, freeze-dried ice cream just didn't quite cut it. Unused to the hard ground, no one slept very well. *Surely,* we thought, *tomorrow will be better.*

It wasn't. It was cold and rainy. Everyone's feet hurt. Then, while hiking up a hill, Libby fell and the boys laughed at her. Where was brotherly compassion? My husband groaned under the weight of all the stuff I had thought we would need. Where were those wonderful deep conversations we were suppose to be having? No one felt like talking.

As we set up camp the second night, it began to thunder. Duchess was afraid of storms, so we zipped her into the tent to sleep with us. It stormed all night long. Rain poured into the tent and soaked our sleeping bags. Every time the dog shook, she sprayed us with cold water. To escape from the dampness, ticks and worms crawled up the tent. Whenever lightning flashed, we gazed up at a covering of disgusting creatures.

Finally at 4 A.M. my wise husband decided enough was enough. He hiked to the road, hitchhiked home to get the car, and came to rescue us.

In the years since, we've had a lot of fun recalling that disastrous camping experience. My children have really enjoyed teasing me. And no, we haven't tried it again. But we have had other times and other kinds of adventures together to nurture our family friendships.

So, even if your attempts at family bonding seem to backfire . . . *you can still become a family of friends.*

No matter where you are in your family life today, you *can* become a family marked by close, loving, supportive relationships. In the next chapter, you will discover how to begin.

Focus Questions

Reflect on your own story.

1. What family friendships would you like to develop?
2. In which relationships do you feel you have experienced close family friendships?
3. What made these relationships especially good?

Family Friendship Builder

Make a picture board in your kitchen. Put photos of your immediate and extended family on the board. Take turns each day praying for the people in one picture.

CHAPTER 2

A Vision
for Your Family

So, do not fear, for I am with you;
do not be dismayed for I am your God.
I will strengthen you and help you;
I will uphold you with my righteous hand.

Isaiah 41:10

On a bleak, rainy day in 1904, Jenny Butchart stood atop a rock at the rim of a quarry and gazed 50 feet below to the quarry floor. Pieces of rock and stagnant puddles were everywhere. For the past 15 years her husband's company in Victoria, British Columbia, Canada, had been excavating limestone and clay from this pit for the manufacture of cement.

The quarry was stark . . . ugly. But Jenny had an idea . . . a dream . . . a vision. She would plant a garden here. It would be the most wonderful garden on earth. When she looked at the ugly, gray rock below her, she envisioned acres and acres of brightly colored flowers, lush green lawns, and still ponds reflecting a blue sky.

"You can't get anything to grow here, Jenny," her friends told her. "Besides, you know nothing about gardening."

But her dream persisted, and when a friend gave her a few sweet pea seeds and a single rose bush, she planted them and went on dreaming. From this modest beginning—a few seeds and a rose bush—her vision began to be fulfilled.

From the very beginning, the work was hard. It was necessary to remove rock debris. Workers brought in tons of top soil from neighboring farms by horse cart. Jennie turned a portion of the quarry into a shimmering lake fed by a waterfall and a stream. Each tree site was meticulously chosen. Each plant was carefully placed and cared for. Jenny wanted harmony in her garden and understood that every plant, tree, or shrub would contribute to that harmony and to the overall beauty of the garden. *Everything* was important.

Today, more than 90 years later, it is difficult to prepare oneself for the overwhelming beauty of Butchart Garden on Vancouver Island. Huge beds of bright red begonias backed by proud yellow zinnias reach out to greet one who passes by. A plume of water soars into the air from a fountain set in the sunken garden. Once bare and gray, the stone quarry walls are now draped with ivy.

Just when you think you can't stand any more beauty, there are more surprises. A rose garden of 2,500 bushes in 250 varieties from all over the world waits just around a bend. Rows and rows of baskets filled with pink, yellow, and blue flowers hang above a walkway leading to a sparkling pool crowned with rare water lilies. Fifty acres of gardens with more than 300,000 flowering plants blaze in the glory of a summer day.

This is Jenny's vision in all its wonder and beauty. Although it is an astonishingly beautiful garden, the work of making it better continues. It is never finished; it is never perfect. It is no longer Jenny who plans, and works in, the garden. Now her grandchildren cultivate it and share it with a million people every year.

Jenny's vision to turn an ugly quarry into a beautiful garden is a lot like cultivating a family of friends. We, too, must begin with a vision. We must want to raise a family that truly loves each other. We must want our children to become friends with each other. We must want our children to become friends with us, and as we look toward the future, we must want to have good relationships with our sons-in-law and daughters-in-law and grandchildren. A family whose members truly love one another is something we must all long for—a vision we must hold in our hearts.

God Doesn't Make Mistakes

When we look at our families, we may be discouraged at what we have to work with. It may seem as if we are viewing a large gray pit. The reality of our situation may be miles away from our vision of family togetherness. Instead of loving, supportive relationships, we may see:

- An exhausted mother who wonders, as she separates her two toddlers in battle over a toy, whether her kids will ever learn to get along.
- A young girl on the brink of adolescence who stomps past her mother with a fury in her eyes that seems to say, "I wish you were someone else's mom."
- A dad who struggles to have a meaningful conversation with his teenage son.
- A new mother who longs to share some of her parenting fears with her own mother.
- A mother-in-law who tries to ease the way for a friendship with her daughter-in-law.
- A grandmother who searches for a good relationship with her hyperactive grandson.
- A single parent who is frustrated because she can't "do it all" and who longs for encouragement.
- A young husband and wife, both from divorced families, who wonder if they have any chance of beating the odds to create a happy family life.

We need a vision. How easy it is to focus on where we are and wonder if God has made a mistake. Jenny Butchart could have focused on the ugly and unpleasant sight of the bare quarry. She could have given up. But instead, she kept her vision clearly in mind and went to work on her garden—bit by bit.

We, too, must keep our vision of creating a family of friends clearly in mind. But remember, our vision is not ours alone. It is also that of our heavenly Father. In Him we have the unlimited resources of the universe: His wisdom, His power, and His forgiveness.

We need support. We need fellow believers who will encourage and advise us, who will pick us up when we fail and encourage us when we want to give up. Role models for ourselves and our children are crucial. A supportive church body can be an extended family to us and our children.

~We need daily care. We have to encourage our family friendships every day. Just as it took time for Jenny's plants to grow and make Butchart Garden beautiful, it takes time to grow healthy friendships within the garden of a family. They don't happen overnight.

~We need seasonal care. In Jenny's garden, the beginning of each new season meant change and more hard work. Old plants had to be lifted and replaced with fragile new ones. And each season had its unique challenges—pesky bugs, a late freeze, or too much rain. It also had its own special beauty—tulips in spring, impatiens in summer, and chrysanthemums in fall.

At different seasons of life we face different challenges in our family friendships. For example, when you are parenting a toddler, some days you feel as though you've lost control. The toddler fusses, cries, is angry, does what you tell him not to do, and does nothing you tell him to do. He keeps you so busy that it's hard to feel you've accomplished much throughout the day.

But toddlers are a blessing, too. You are forced to become flexible. You are forced to rediscover that relationships are more important than accomplishments. You are forced to put aside your "to do" lists and concentrate on building a relationship with this child. You will always have lists, but you will not always have this little guy who throws his arms around your neck and says, "I wuv 'u, Mommy."

Just when you figure out how to live with toddlers and young children, they become teenagers. The season of teenage years is one of mood swings and lessening parental control. It can be tricky to know how much to hold on and how much to let go. The gift of this season of life is that you can develop peer friendships with your children.

At each season of the year, Jenny Butchart had to make choices—which plants to highlight, where to put new perennials, and what colors to mix. Sometimes she had a difficult time choosing. Different seasons in family life will also require us to make tough choices.

Making Choices

Today's world offers too many opportunities—too many good things from which to choose. We can spend our time and our money in a million ways. How do we make wise choices for ourselves and our children with so many options? We have to keep in mind our goal of cultivating a family of friends, and at each season of family life, we need to ask the question, "Ten years from now, will the choice I make today have been the best one to help our family members grow in love for one another?"

As children reach the later elementary years, parents have to choose between the many activities in which children can become involved. It isn't always the children who pick too many activities. Our children's over-commitment can be driven by parental peer pressure.

You may be sitting with other parents at a ball game and one of the mothers begins to describe all the activities in which her daughter is involved. Another parent interrupts to describe a club her son has joined. All of a sudden you may feel inadequate because your child isn't doing everything the others are. So the next time your child indicates an interest in an activity, you encourage him to join. Then one more evening of each week is spent eating in shifts and carpooling kids. Slowly you begin to realize that your family members are merely passing in the night and that they are not really connecting with each other.

It's time to call a halt to all activities and reevaluate. The truth is that sitting down to a family dinner together will have a far greater impact on developing family friendships than adding another activity to your child's life.

One friend with a large family has limited her children's activities outside the regular classroom to one per child. Another has told her sons they can choose one sport per year and not one per season.

Each family's choices will be different, but all should ask, "What is realistic for my family? What encourages my vision for cultivating family friendships?" Too often the question is, "How many activities can we pack in?" as opposed to, "Which and how many activities can family members participate in and still have time for family togetherness?"

Not only must we look at our children's activities, we must examine our own as well. We must be wise with our commitments. It's all too easy to get so busy in our careers or volunteer obligations that we are unable to attend a child's soccer game or school play. If we want to have a friendship with our 17-year-old, then we must take time to be at his events when he's seven years old.

The Value of Learning to Wait

One benefit of seeing life in terms of seasons is that we realize there will be some things that we will have to put off until the next season in life.

This is hard, especially for baby-boomers. We believe and expect that we can have it all NOW. We are in a rush to live life to the fullest and are fearful of missing out. We desperately need to learn to wait.

A mother of young children may have to wait for a later season to take college classes. A parent who wishes to travel for a career may need to wait until the kids are grown in order to be at home with teenagers. A couple may need to wait on a financial purchase and use the money for a family vacation where friendships can deepen.

When we experience a change in the seasons of life, it's often wise to wait before accepting new commitments. A mom whose youngest child finally goes off to school may be ecstatic to have free time. Immediately she fills her calendar with appointments and commitments. After a few weeks she is exhausted and more frantic than she was before she gained her freedom.

Then, one day her child becomes ill and she has to cancel a meeting to stay home. "I'm so glad to have an excuse to stay home," she confides to a friend.

Wait a minute! Something is amiss when we must have an excuse to stay home. It might be better for this mom to refrain from making new commitments for the first six months after her last child goes off to school. During this period she will have time to adjust to her new freedom and to gain a better perspective on how to make wise decisions for this new season in her life.

With three teenagers still at home, John and I have little time for a social life with our peers. Instead, when we have free time, we prefer spending it with our kids, playing tennis or just having their friends to the house. In a few years when our kids are gone, we'll socialize with our own friends.

A vision, support, and daily and seasonal care are all necessary for building family friendships. But one more thing is needed: tools. Without tools, Jenny's garden would never have come into being. Tools are essential to giving birth to your vision. The purpose of this book is to provide you with the necessary tools for cultivating friendships within your family.

There is some frustration in writing a book like this because each chapter could be a book by itself. But because each family relationship impacts another, it is important to examine the whole. As you read this book, I hope you will discover a fresh vision for family friendship and learn to use the tools to make your vision a reality.

You will benefit most if you read the book one chapter at a time and then pause to reflect on what you have read. Take time to consider the questions at the end of each chapter. Resist the temptation to read a chapter out of context or to turn to the chapter that represents the current season of your life. The chapters of this book are like a family. They are interrelated and interdependent. Each chapter depends on the others for full understanding and meaning. The stories in the book are all true, but some of the names have been changed to protect individuals' privacy.

Our society cries out with the pain of broken relationships. Parents who bear the wounds of their own past are searching for ways to break the cycles of woundedness. They need to know that their families can be the first of a long line of healthy families. They need to know they can start a new cycle.

Parents from strong, healthy homes also face the challenge of building strong relationships within their families. Our culture highlights violence, unfaithfulness, drugs, and disease. Our children are exposed to things of which we never dreamed. The pace of life today pulls families apart. There are too many things to do and too little time to do them. Stress has become a national plague. Our culture makes becoming a family of friends a challenge for each of us.

People everywhere long for someone who cares, for someone who will be there in life's ups and downs, for a family that works. Everyone is looking for some sign of hope.

As your family friendships grow, I pray your family will become a beacon of hope, lighting the way for those who have lost theirs in a broken world.

Focus Questions

Meditate on Colossians 3:12-17.

1. Paul tells us to put on or live out several qualities. These are traits that we all want to see in our own families. What are they?
2. Describe each of these traits in your own words. How does each characteristic apply to family friendships?
3. What trait do you most want to grow in this year?

Family Friendship Builder

ˎ Reflecting on these traits, write a letter to God describing the family relationships that you want Him to develop in your family. Share the areas that you especially desire to grow in this year. Across the bottom of your letter write out the promise in Isaiah 41:10.

PART TWO

What Does It Take to Make a Family of Friends?

Security:
The Foundation for
Family Friendships

"As for me, this is my covenant with them," says the Lord.
"My Spirit, which is on you, and my words which I have put in
your mouth will not depart from your mouth, or from the mouths of
your children, or from the mouths of their descendants
from this time on and forever," says the Lord.
Isaiah 59:21

We'd been married only a few months, and we were having a serious argument. I was devastated. My eyes were puffy from crying, and my emotions seemed to race from anger to fear. *How could this be happening?* I asked myself. *We were so in love.* This argument, however, seemed to be acute and neither of us was willing to give in. Finally, in total frustration, I looked at John and said, "Well, maybe we shouldn't have gotten married in the first place!"

My normally even-tempered husband stood up, and with a conviction tinged with righteous anger he looked me straight in the eye and replied, "Don't you ever, *ever* say that again! We are married, period!" And I've never said it again.

What my husband gave me with that one statement was an undergirding sense of security. Our marriage was not to be questioned. In the context of that security, we eventually resolved our disagreement. That argument and subsequent ones were pretty much forgotten. What I remember is his statement of commitment.

At that fearful moment of questioning, what I needed most was a reminder that he did not doubt our marriage relationship, that we were committed for life. And that was what he gave me.

Sadly, marriage vows and family life aren't very secure today. In Washington, D.C., one of the most popular seminars being held is about how to write prenuptial contracts. The purpose of these contracts is to provide the least painful way to dissolve marriage. More and more people seem to view marriage as a legal contract between two people that lasts until one person becomes unhappy. Then it is nullified.

God's design for marriage and family has never been a contract that can be easily broken. Instead, He desires marriage to be a covenant made before Him and others that is a permanent, unconditional agreement between two imperfect people and Himself. It does not ensure a perfect relationship, but does require a lasting and holy one.

A covenant is one of the oldest forms of agreement. It is the most powerful concept in the Bible because it pictures God Himself entering into a relationship with human beings. God entered into covenants with Noah, Abraham, and David—covenants to be faithful to them and their descendants forever.

In Genesis 2, we see a very clear picture of the establishment of the marriage covenant when God brought Adam and Eve together. God presided over their marriage and joined them together in perfect union. Even though Adam and Eve gave themselves unreservedly to each other, God was still very much at the center of their commitment. And even when they were unfaithful to Him, God was still faithful to them.

So, from the biblical point of view, marriage is not simply a human commitment of two people to each other, but a triangle partnership between a man, a woman, and God. Every Christian marriage ceremony is a reenactment of this first marriage. Husbands and wives make their promises to one another and to God, and they ask for His blessing and participation in the marriage.

This covenant relationship is not limited to the two participants in the marriage, but is extended to their offspring, who are children of the covenant. Extended families on both sides are also recognized as part of the covenant union.

Understanding our family relationships in the context of a covenant gives us a tremendous sense of security. We no longer see ourselves linked merely by human agreement, but by a promise made before man and God in which God Himself has participated. Every believing couple is a triangle with God at the apex, and every family is a little church. But in today's world there are clearly several threats to the covenant concept of family.

Threats That Disrupt Security

You No Longer Meet My Needs

An attractive woman with several young children was thrilled when her husband landed a high-level government job in Washington, D.C. Both were committed believers, and over the years they had prayed about his career path. Now their prayers seemed to be answered. Thrust into the limelight with his challenging job, the husband began to spend longer and longer hours at the office. He rarely found time for his wife and children. Concerned friends challenged him about his habits, but his answer was always, "You just don't understand. What I'm doing is so important."

As time went by, his professional successes increased and his family life decreased. Caught up in a world of self-importance, he soon found another woman who he felt met his needs more effectively than his wife, and another family fell apart.

We've Tried Everything

A young couple, married barely a year, began to have trouble—serious trouble. Finally, she left and went home to her folks. He didn't want her to come back. It seemed the whole marriage had been a big mistake. Family members offered her compassion and love and encouraged her to put the past behind her and to begin again. But when she phoned her minister, he told her to go back to her husband and fight for her marriage. "You made a promise before God," he said, "and it's worth fighting for. In 10 years, you'll want to look back and say, 'I did everything I could to make my marriage work.'"

So she went back. It was very difficult; she tried everything and she prayed. Slowly, over the next year, positive changes began to take place in both her husband's life and in her life. Now, several years later, they are happier than they have ever been. God has the power to change people's lives and rebuild broken marriages.

You Aren't Living the Way I Raised You

Our friend's marriage was a mess and finally his wife left him and their daughter. He truly loved his daughter, and he raised her in the best way he could. But when she was almost grown, the unacceptable happened. After months of dating a man of whom her father did not approve, she married him. When her father heard the news, he exploded with anger. "I would rather she had died!" he exclaimed.

"But she's still your daughter," I said. "And her children will be your grandchildren. What's done is done. You must leave a path open for a relationship with her."

A year later, he still has not spoken to her. If either the father or the daughter were to die, there would be only regrets.

Threats to the covenant come in many different forms. We've talked about only three of many kinds. What do we do about physical, mental, or emotional abuse? Does God understand our pain?

God does, indeed, understand our pain. He aches with us and weeps for us and our children. He hates the pain that family members experience because of any kind of abuse. There are cases where leaving seems to be the only option for the health and safety of a family.

We know that while such cases happen, divorce is not God's perfect will. Those who have already experienced it understand why. They, perhaps even more than others, long for healthy marriages and healthy parent-child relationships for their own children. They long for a life lived within the security of the covenant.

Because there are so many threats to the covenant of marriage, it is important to understand the many strengths it provides. Appreciating these strengths will enable us to establish an atmosphere of security within our homes that will encourage strong friendships and provide confidence and assurance for our children.

Security-Producing Strengths of a Covenant

A Covenant Means Lifelong Commitment

The way in which John handled our first, devastating argument was a vivid reminder of the lifelong commitment we had made to our marriage and to each other. It also alleviated my tendency to panic and to think, *Oh no! We're going to become one of those statistics—couples that don't make it.* When I could fall back on the covenant of our marriage, I was reassured about the permanence of our relationship. And we were forced to work out our differences and to get things straight.

We must view all of family life as a covenant relationship. When we do, we cannot become emotionally divorced from other family members. My friend who was furious with his daughter could have received hope from the covenant of family. God is able to give them a new relationship; but to receive it, this father will have to reach out to his daughter.

Whether wives, fathers, or children, we must be committed to our family members forever. We must work through our difficulties with them. This is not bad, for our difficulties provide us with a choice. We can see them as devastating or as providing opportunities to grow and learn more about ourselves, our family members, and our Lord.

Living under a covenant means we are willing to go the extra mile to build a relationship. Pride will keep us from covenant living. It's good to remember the lesson of the Jewish father welcoming home his prodigal son. Our homes should have a "welcome mat" that says, "No matter what you've done, you are welcome here."

It's not enough to embrace a covenant philosophy for your marriage; it is important to explain to your children what a covenant is and what it means to the marriage and to the family. My friends were having a huge argument when their children walked into the room. Turning to his kids, the dad said, "We're not getting a divorce. We're having an argument. We will work it out."

Our children need the reassurance of hearing us express our commitment to the covenant we've made—a covenant that says, "We are married for life." They are surrounded by broken relationships. Friends, relatives, and parents divorce. They see it every day, so don't assume that your children feel secure about your home and relationship.

Nan and Larry have been in the military for years. A strong Christian couple committed to the covenant of marriage, they have a wonderful family life. At the different military posts where they have lived, their housing has always been tight, with just enough bedrooms for family members. However, on one particular move when their daughters were young, they were able to purchase a large home with an extra bedroom. Nan couldn't understand it when the girls were visibly upset about having a guest bedroom.

It took some sensitive digging, but she finally got the girls to tell her that they were afraid their parents were not getting along and might get divorced. Their friend's parents had moved into separate bedrooms and then divorced. They feared that if their parents wanted an extra bedroom, it was because they no longer wanted to be together. Nan was stunned, to say the least, but that experience reminds us all of the intense fear our children have of a family breakup. Because they are surrounded by it, they need constant reassurance that their parents' marriage is for life.

Let your children see you working on your marriage. Go on dates together. Take time for marriage enrichment classes. Get counseling if it is needed. Take time to cultivate your marriage friendship. Your kids are learning how to be married as they watch you.

The lifelong commitment of covenant needs to be emphasized not only in our marriages, but also in our commitment to our children. I remember my dad saying to me frequently, "Susan, no matter what you do or where you go, I want you to know that I'll always be there for you." That's commitment!

Yes, we need to live it, but we also need to say it. Silence can be negative, and there are many children who have never heard their dad or mom say, "Son, I love you, and although I will not always agree with you or approve of what you do, I'll always love you and I'll always be here for you."

This kind of commitment provides a sense of belonging that, in turn, produces security and enables the building of family friendships.

A Covenant Allows for Failure

Don and Linda are our friends. He has a leadership position in a large evangelical church. Their children are believers, and as a family they have had a positive impact on many people. But some time ago their daughter went through a difficult time—a time when she would not listen to anyone. She was dating a boy who did not share her faith. Soon she became pregnant. When she told her parents, they were devastated. Anger, hurt, and guilt overwhelmed them. They had warned her again and again. They had made clear God's teaching on the sanctity of sex. They had raised her in a loving Christian home.

"Where have we gone wrong with this precious child?" they asked themselves. It was a very painful time for them. While they did not approve of what she had done, she was still their daughter, and so they stood beside her. She broke up with the boy, went through much counseling to decide whether to give the baby up for adoption or to keep it. Her parents supported her by leaving the decision in her hands. When she decided to keep the baby, they were there for her. Her mom even went through the delivery with her. And as she began to raise her baby girl, they encouraged her. After a while, she recommitted her life to Christ and began to grow in her faith.

Out of painful failure, a family grew closer, and the picture of two parents' covenant commitment to their child was a great lesson for the community.

In another town Jack was struggling. Unhappy at home and unfulfilled at work, he soon found himself pouring out his heart to a female coworker. His emotional attraction soon became physical, and he became involved in an affair. His wife was furious and his children were torn apart. Jack himself was miserable. It seemed like another marriage was about to become history and another family destroyed.

But his wife determined that she would take her marriage vows seriously and stick with him. It took many months and much counseling, but today when I see them in church together, I am challenged by this woman's commitment to the covenant. She *would not* give up, even in the face of seeming failure. And the new relationship that God has brought out of such pain is indeed a treasure.

A Covenant Provides Room to Grow

I was four years old when my brother was born. Being the first child and quite used to having my own way, I did not adjust well to this intrusion into my territory. When my second brother arrived two years later, I was furious. I even refused to speak to my mother when she came home from the hospital. After all, she wasn't bringing me a sister but another brother. In my mind, that was a disaster!

For years, I really did not like either of the boys. They took my parents' time, their room was always a mess, and they always seemed to be dirty. Besides all that, there were two of them and one of me.

I was 10 by the time my sister was born, and I was far more interested in my own friends than in having a baby sister. I was definitely not sweet to my siblings. To say that I was friends with my younger brothers and sister would have been a great exaggeration. Yet, today, we are best of friends.

What happened?

Time passed; we grew up. My parents did many things right in those early years that enabled strong friendships to develop, but they did not see the results of their efforts for several years. (In chapter 10, we'll look at specific steps we can take to build sibling friendships.) The most important thing they gave us was the sense that we were a family and we were committed to one another for life. We were secure in knowing we had *time* to become friends. That was encouraging during those periods when we didn't get along.

My two young nieces are 15 months apart. Their temperaments are very different, and they're constantly at odds with one another. Often their home feels like a war zone. It is often very discouraging for the parents and the girls as well. But their mom says to them, "Girls, we have to keep working at this. You are sisters for life and that is the greatest gift you can have, even though you don't believe it right now. One day you *will* like each other. When you get older, you will find that you are friends." Then she prays for their relationship and helps them work on it one day at a time with an eye toward the future.

In the same way that knowing our marriages are for life provides us with room to grow, knowing that we are a family, forever, allows us to encourage friendships with and between our children. That sense of commitment causes us not to give up on one another.

A Covenant Means Our Ultimate Security Is in Christ

We were in tears. Our son's friend's dad had just announced that he did not love his wife anymore and was leaving. He had found someone else. There had been no hint of trouble. He seemed like the perfect husband and dad, never missing his son's baseball games and always in church with his family. His wife was shocked and his children devastated. And then he was gone. His communication with his kids became infrequent and his financial support almost nonexistent.

It has been nearly 10 years since he left. These have been hard years for the family, but I have watched my friend and her children grow in their faith. They know that their real security is in Christ—the only One who will never leave them nor forsake them (Heb. 13:5).

The covenant relationship we have within our families isn't perfect. We may be parted by tragedy, by death, by circumstances not of our own making. Our children need the security of their parents' marriage and of their parents' commitment to them. But most of all, they need parents whose security is in God.

We must not try to be the ultimate security for our kids. Giving kids security doesn't mean rescuing them. It may mean the more difficult task of letting them go and watching them make mistakes. For, ultimately, they must be responsible for their own actions. Their security cannot be in Mom or Dad, but in God alone.

Our goal is to steadily turn our children away from their earthly parents, who will let them down, toward a heavenly Father who will always be there for them and in whose arms they will always be secure.

Living under a covenant with our mates and children provides us with a mirror image of the perfect security that we can have in Christ. When I look in the mirror, I notice that my nose is too big. It looks distorted. The imperfections in the glass make my face look misshapen. A film of dust graciously hides a blemish on my face. And yet I know the reflection staring back from the glass is me. It's not the *real* me, but it's the best likeness of me there is. Our family relationships are an imperfect reflection of God's perfect relationship with us.

ʻIt works like this. I love my husband even though sometimes I don't like him very much. My kids are my greatest treasures, although at times I've wished someone else would take them for a while. But if anyone tried to harm my children or my husband, I would become an angry tigress. Even though my love is not perfect, and my commitment sometimes gets wobbly, my family is mine and I love them.

God's commitment to us is the real thing. It's perfect and without blemish. His covenant lasts forever. No one nor no thing can distort it. His love and commitment to you, to me, and to our children is the most, at this very moment, that it can ever be. It is in His flawless covenant that we must find our ultimate security.

Focus Questions

Meditate on 1 Peter 1:3-9.

1. Verses 3-6 remind us of several things that we have been given by God. What are they? How secure are they?

2. When we face difficulties similar to those in verses 6-9, how can we be comforted?
3. What promise in these verses do we need to focus on today? Write it out in your own words and tape it to the refrigerator.

Family Friendship Builder

A true friend is someone you can count on. Make a list of everything that God gives us in our friendship relationship with Him. Using a concordance, find and list verses describing these things. For example: He always gives me hope (1 Pet. 1:3) and only He will never leave me (Heb. 13:5).

CHAPTER 4

Encouragement: The Helping Hand for Family Friendships

*May our Lord Jesus Christ himself and God our Father,
who loved us and by his grace gave us eternal encouragement
and good hope, encourage your hearts and strengthen you
in every good deed and word.*

2 Thessalonians 2:16, 17

Hurrying home from school, the little guy slammed the front door and tossed his papers on the floor. Then he noticed the letter propped on the hall table—the place of prominence for important messages. Looking closely, he saw with surprise that it was addressed to him. He could hardly restrain himself as he began to tear open the letter.

Hey Brother,

I'm so glad you're coming up Saturday to see me. I'll feel like it's part my birthday, too. Hope you had a nice party Friday afternoon. Didn't we have the greatest time together when Mom and Dad went away? Remember how we went to the ball game and all the questions you asked and all the ice cream cones we had? And remember how you and Sammy and I went swimming? Boy, I really enjoyed that weekend! And you only wet the bed once— of course, that time you nearly drowned both of us!

I just want you to know that I think that you're the greatest little brother a guy could ever hope to have—a brother who's so honest and fair at all times. And when something bothers you, you just say, "Now, God, I don't know what to do. I want you to take this and work it all out for the best." And boy, He will too! Aren't we glad that God loves us so?

Hope you are getting along fine in school. I'm so glad I went over and saw your new school. It surely is fine and pretty. I know you like your teacher lots. I remember how I enjoyed third grade so much. I know you will too.

Looking forward to seeing you on Saturday. Eight years old! I just can't believe it. You are really growing up. Be a good boy and look after everything for me.

Much love,
Your brother

This older brother taught him to throw a baseball and to ride horseback. He gave him special books, read the Bible with him, and prayed with him, always treating him as an equal. The relationship they established went on, and when the younger brother's college sweetheart dumped him for someone else, his big brother comforted him. Years later, when he was married, had a bunch of kids, and was financially strapped, his big brother bought him an automobile. Did the encouragement of a brother who was 10 years older have an impact on this little boy? It certainly did. That little boy became my husband, John Yates.

We all have a great need for encouragement. A well-known actress once said, "We live by encouragement, we die without it, slowly, sadly, and angrily." Life is difficult and we need to know that someone believes in us, loves us no matter what happens, will be there to pick us up when we fail, will forgive us again and again, and will cheer us on when we are fearful.

Friendships are nurtured by the steady give and take of encouragement. The family should be the primary provider of this nutrient. In a family, we are accepted not because of what we have done or have not done, but simply because we are family.

Just as the soil in Jenny Butchart's garden had to contain specific ingredients for her flowers to be healthy and to flourish, we must make sure our family life has elements that will produce an atmosphere of encouragement. For when family members are encouraged, the bonds of friendship between them are strengthened. Four ingredients will provide a healthy atmosphere in which encouragement can blossom.

Ingredient One: We Are Open with Each Other

My friend Bette was in tears. As a single mother of a six-year-old son, she was struggling financially, suffering from loneliness, and wondering just how she was going to raise her boy alone. One day her young son found her crying. Knowing some of her specific concerns, he gently put his hand on his mom's shoulder and said, "Mom, did you pray yet?"

The blunt reminder shook Bette with the realization that she was not alone. She had a heavenly Father who cared about every concern of hers. Hugging her child, she said, "You're right. Let's pray together."

Several years later it was the son who was in tears. There was a father-son banquet at their church, and he had no father to take him. He openly shared his pain with his mother, for she had always been open with him. This time she comforted *him* and then they prayed together. Several days later a man from the church phoned to ask if the child would go with him as his "adopted" son.

Even if the phone call had never come, a young boy and a thankful mother would still have grown deeper in friendship with each other as they together took their pain to their heavenly Father.

Bette knew the importance of being open with her child, and because of her transparency, her son found it easy to be open with her in return. Some people find it easy to be vulnerable, while others keep a tight lid on what is really going on inside. As parents, we have to be willing to take the first step toward openness and give our children time to respond in their own way and at their own pace. Giving them time sometimes means we must simply listen and not offer advice.

The hassled mother of young children who has spent her entire day breaking up fights, cleaning house, feeding kids, and not accomplishing anything on her "list" greets her husband at the door and bursts into tears. She doesn't need him to come up with a new time-management plan for her. Instead, she needs a big hug and a husband who says, "I think you are the most wonderful wife in the world. You have the hardest job there is with these kids. I don't know how you do what you do!" And she needs him to listen . . . period. Listening is the biggest encouragement he can give her.

There are times when just listening works and there are other times when the best encouragement *is* the giving of advice. Andy was having a hard time in school. Just back from a Christian camp, he was excited about his faith, but none of his friends seemed to share his enthusiasm. Yes, they were believers, but they wanted to have a little fun, too. Because he did not want to join in some of their partying, Andy found himself alone and left out.

"I'm so lonely," he said to his mom. "It's not fair and it's so hard."

She listened for a few minutes and then asked, "Son, do you think I've ever been lonely?"

He thought and then replied, "Yeah, I guess you were when we lived in the mountains and you had no friends close by."

"That's right. I learned during that experience that I had to rely on the Lord, and although it was hard, it became a time of real growth for me. Sometimes loneliness draws us closer to God." With tears in her eyes, she gave her son a hug and said, "I can feel your pain, but I can't fix it. Use this time to draw close to God."

Sometime later Andy remarked to his mother that he was thankful he had had to learn that being God's man was more important than whether or not he was lonely.

When encouragement is needed, we have to ask God for help in how best to respond. Should we simply comfort and listen, or is it appropriate to give advice? When offering encouragement, sometimes we get it right and sometimes we don't. It's not easy to know for sure, but if we take a few minutes to think before we act, we'll be more likely to respond in a way that encourages others.

When we are trying to cultivate an atmosphere of openness, it's important to be up front about what may be causing our moodiness. For a long time my husband seemed grumpy on Saturdays. I couldn't figure out why. Didn't he like spending time with the kids and me? What was wrong?

Had the kids done something? Had I? When the pattern continued for some time, we talked and I told him I couldn't understand why he seemed so unpleasant on Saturdays. He didn't realize he had been communicating grumpiness. We finally figured out that he felt pressure because he was unprepared for his Sunday sermons.

Now when he's unprepared he says, "Gang, I want you to know that if I'm on edge today, it's not because of you. I'm not upset with any of you. You are a great family. It's just that my sermon isn't right." What a great relief to be told that you are not the cause of someone's bad mood.

When the twins were colicky, nursing babies, the boys were two and four years old, and Allison was seven, I didn't get much sleep. By late afternoon each day, it was all I could do just to function. Believe me, I wasn't enthusiastic or encouraging. And sometimes the bigger kids wondered, *Is Mom mad?* I learned to tell them when I was very tired. It wasn't that I was upset with them. They were great kids, but I was tired.

It isn't fair to make family members guess what's going on inside you. They'll tend to assume you disapprove of them. Isn't it better, whenever possible, to communicate the reason for your mood? And if you can't tell them what's wrong, at least communicate that the problem is yours and you are not upset because of something they did or said.

Open talks don't happen automatically. We have to pay attention and be sensitive to those times when family members are ready for a deeper level of communication. My friend Ann noticed that when she curled up on the couch by the fireplace with a roaring fire going and her teenage son nearby, he seemed to unwind and become more communicative.

Bedtime is a natural moment for conversation. You may hear things at bedtime that you never thought you would. It's a great time for sharing, because the child doesn't want to go to sleep. Take advantage of it and have a few minutes of special talk before you firmly say good night.

Some men seem to communicate best while working on a project. A father and son I know have great conversations while working on a car together. Women, however, don't seem to need any props. They communicate with ease simply by being together.

Openness takes time and patience, and we need to have a long-range view of what we hope to accomplish. We need to remind ourselves that the best things often take a long time to happen.

Ingredient Two: Appreciate One Another

When our children were small, one of our favorite family games was "Spin the Bottle." We would take an old bottle, sit in a circle, and one person would spin the bottle until it stopped and pointed to someone. The spinner then shared with that person something she appreciated about him. Then the person to whom the bottle had pointed took the next turn to spin.

I still remember some of the appreciations handed out during those games. Once, one of the twins appreciated Allison because she let her sleep with her when she was scared and didn't get too mad when she wet Allison's bed! One of the other kids appreciated me for carpooling. Dad was appreciated for reading at bedtimes, and one of the boys appreciated his little sister because she gave good hugs. Our game was always a time of encouragement.

Although we no longer play "Spin the Bottle," our family continues the tradition of encouragement in different ways. One of those is just telling the person seated to the right at mealtime something he or she does that you appreciate. On birthdays family members take a few minutes to tell the honorees what they appreciate most about them.

Our tendency in life is to take others for granted rather than to express appreciation. Our family has found these simple activities helpful in rekindling a thankful spirit.

Asking advice of others indicates that you appreciate and value their opinions. My girls have a good eye for clothes and very definite opinions about what I should wear—especially to *their* functions! Recently, they agreed that I could go to a talent show at their school as long as they got to pick out what I wore! Rarely, now, do I purchase anything without their approval. I appreciate their help and opinions on my wardrobe.

Often, one family member may seem to need lots of encouragement. He may thrive on it. There may be another person who doesn't seem to need much encouragement. It's easy to neglect this one and not show appreciation for him because his need isn't as obvious. But remember, he still has a need.

One of my children is more laid back than the others. It's easy to assume he is doing just fine, but it struck me some time ago he needed some special attention even though he didn't say so. I bought a loaf of his favorite cinnamon bread and put it on his pillow with a little note telling him some specific things that I appreciate about him. Later he said, "Hey,

Mom, thanks for the bread and the note." He didn't rave on and on, but I knew it meant a lot to him. It was a good reminder for me to not take *anyone* for granted.

What do we do if we are giving appreciation to other folks and are getting no response? Keep doing it! Jesus says we are to keep forgiving, so surely we can keep appreciating. Perhaps estranged in-laws don't respond to our appreciation of them. We never hear from them and our relationship is nil. Just keep sending notes. Just keep remembering birthdays. Send cards for no reason. Even though we have no idea when, or if, they will respond, we must keep on building the bridge. Our behavior cannot be dictated by the responses we get. We have to go on doing acts of appreciation and kindness simply because it is right.

Ingredient Three: Support Each Other

A well-to-do family has a lovely house filled with many beautiful possessions. Antiques, oriental rugs, valuable paintings, and beautiful silver characterize this lovely home. In one corner of the den sits a big, comfortable chair. It's Dad's special chair. When he comes into the room, he always sits there. But the chair is more than just a place to sit. It's "Dad's cuddling chair." It has always been the place where Dad sits with his children in his lap, hugging them, telling them how much he loves them, and talking to them. Secrets are told, tears are shed, and giggles overflow from this special chair. What do you think will happen when Dad and Mom have died? Will it be the silver or the paintings that each child wants the most? No, it will be "Dad's cuddling chair." An old chair and the dad who took time to use it wisely have had a far greater impact on building family friendships than all the other material possessions of this family put together.

The gift of time is the bottom line in communicating support. Much has been made over the "quality versus quantity time" needs of our families. *Both* are needed. Small children don't need big hunks of time; rather, they need minutes here and there that can be used to create traditions like a cuddling chair.

Did you know that you cannot schedule quality time to have a deep talk with a teenager? Teenagers are most likely to be in the mood for a deep talk when it suits you the least. More often than not, you must simply hang out and be available for a deep talk with your teen whenever the mood strikes! If you are spending *quantity* time with your teenager, it will encourage more of those tender moments of *quality* communication.

But no matter what you do, none of us ever feels we have spent enough time with our mates or our children.

Another way of showing support is by attending other family members' special events. When you cancel a meeting to attend your daughter's soccer game, you are showing your support for her. Without words, it communicates how important she is to you. When you attend a lecture your wife is giving or go to a presentation that your husband is making, you are saying, "I'm interested in you and in what you do."

Encourage support by getting older kids to attend the younger ones' events. Younger kids always get dragged to the big kids' events. Sometimes they need the support of their older siblings. You, as a parent, may have to insist that your older son attend at least one of his little sister's ball games even if she sits on the bench the whole game. Our families must serve as personal cheerleaders for one another, not just at ball games, but at all the events of life. This is important in building family friendships.

Bragging about each other is a wonderful means of offering support. A father of teenagers recently said to his children, "We are so lucky that Mom is willing to run an open house. She has a real gift of making people feel at home when they come here."

In another family, a younger sister remarked to a visiting family member, "My big brother is so nice to all my friends. He always speaks to them in the hall at school and that makes me feel so good."

In supporting one another it is helpful to employ the "clue in" principle. Perhaps a teen is blue because she has not been invited to a school concert. Mom can clue in a younger sister and have her write Big Sis a love note and leave it with a treat on her pillow. A quick call to Dad before he comes home from work to let him know "we have a moody teen tonight" can prepare him for what he will encounter at home and alert him to be especially sensitive or to grant some space as the need may be. A big part of a parent's role is noticing needs and clueing in family members as to how they might be supportive.

Ingredient Four: Believe in One Another

At age four, Sammy was struggling with a speech deficit. He attended weekly speech classes, but both he and his parents were frustrated because he didn't seem to be making much progress. For days he struggled with saying *balloon* correctly. It always came out *babloon*. His mouth just wouldn't cooperate with his head.

Finally, his older brother sat down with him. "Sammy," he said, "I know you can do it. Look at my lips and let's do it together." After many attempts and much encouragement from his big brother, little Sammy finally blurted out *balloon*.

His excited brother called the rest of the family into the room, and they clapped as Sammy said *balloon* over and over again. A patient older brother believed that his little brother could make progress and was willing to stick with him and cheer for him until he did.

In families, people must have the freedom to fail. No one will be good at everything he attempts. In fact, it's important to discover your weaknesses. Allow your children the freedom to experiment with different interests. A child might try tennis because her parents are avid players and discover that she doesn't have a natural aptitude nor does she like the sport. That's okay. She may be gifted in the arts and desire to take an art class. Encourage your children to experiment with various kinds of activities to see what most suits them.

One 14-year-old girl was a tiger on the soccer field. Yet, in one particular game, she played poorly and her team lost. Dejected and downcast, she walked slowly off the playing field. Her older brother met her and, putting his arms around her, said, "Hey, Sis, it's okay! I had some rotten games in my day, too. You're a great player and I know you'll do better next time."

Friendships in a family grow as we believe in one another and stick with each other through the hard times. As parents, we must encourage our children to reach out to one another and give them specific ways in which they can do this. It might be you who tells your older son to meet his sister when she comes off the soccer field. You may have to suggest what he might say to her that will encourage her. In the beginning, it may not be natural for children to do this. Our job as parents is to train our children and show them how to be supportive, encouraging, and friendly with siblings, trusting that one day they will begin to do it on their own.

We must remember two things as we seek to believe in each other. Remember that people change and remember to maintain a sense of humor. The shy child who is afraid to speak up in class may one day become the student council president. It happens! A boy in our town who struggled with learning disabilities for years began to improve and then to excel. By the end of high school, his improvement was so great that he graduated with many awards and was accepted into a prestigious engineering school where he is now designing machinery.

Family friends avoid words like *always* and *never*. Phrases such as "You'll never learn to do this" or "You always mess up at this" cause those who are struggling to lose hope that they can ever change.

A sense of humor appropriately shared will have a way of reducing embarrassment and a feeling of failure. We must first learn to laugh at our own mistakes and not take life so seriously. Then, by putting our arms around a dejected family member and laughing together over something he has done, we can restore perspective and lessen his disappointment.

My parents were always great at communicating that they believed in me. Often Mom or Dad would say, "Susan, there's nothing you can't do if you just set your mind to it." Their belief in me got me through some hard times when I could not believe in myself. Mom's and Dad's ultimate faith was in God, but their belief in me provided me with a security that made friendship with them and with my heavenly Father natural.

A letter from a big brother, a hug in Dad's cuddling chair, a mom who tells her children she believes in them, and a family that cheers at little steps of progress all contribute to an atmosphere of encouragement that will strengthen the bonds of friendship within the family.

Focus Questions

Read and meditate on Philemon.

1. This short letter gives us insight into three people: Paul, Philemon, and Onesimus. What is the relationship between the three?
2. How has Philemon encouraged Paul? List specific ways.
3. List specific things that Paul says that encourage Philemon as he asks him a special favor. What attitude does he communicate?
4. Pray and ask God to make you an encourager of people.

Family Friendship Builder

Choose someone in your immediate or extended family who needs encouragement. Write a note and tell him what he means to you and what you appreciate about him.

CHAPTER 5

Respect: The Place of Honor in Family Friendships

"He who fears (or respects) the Lord
has a secure fortress, and for his children
it will be a refuge."

Proverbs 14:26, parentheses added

A young mother decided that she needed to have a serious talk with her daughter. At six years of age, the girl was becoming increasingly hateful to her younger brother. They rarely got along, and my exhausted friend felt more like a referee than a mother. Sitting on her daughter's bed one night, she explained to her that ugly talk was no longer permitted in the house. The children were not allowed to say "Shut up" or "I hate you" to one another. She explained that such words were unkind and unacceptable.

After a few minutes of listening intently, the child looked at her mother and asked, "Mom, does this mean you won't say those things to Dad anymore?"
Ouch!

My friend realized that her daughter was right and that she had to change if respect was to be a reality in their home. She readily made the adjustment because she knew that in order to build friendships among family members, she, too, had to be consistent with her own rules for how family members were to be treated.

Recently, at an opening assembly of our public high school, the principal gave a two-minute speech. Before the entire student body and faculty, he said simply, "If this year each of us determines to have self-respect, to respect property, and to respect one another, we will have a great year."

A wise leader once said, "Dishonesty, disobedience, and disrespect should not be accepted in our homes." Respect is a vital ingredient in building strong friendships. It's hard to have a deep relationship with someone whom you do not respect. And training in respect begins in the home.

Maintain Clear Standards with Consistent Discipline

We were standing in line at a wedding reception when Ginny began to share with me her frustrations in training her three young children.

"Susan," she said, "I feel like I'm always disciplining them and I never seem to get anywhere. I continually have to break up fights, punish them for back talk, and remind them over and over to be thoughtful. I'm beginning to wonder if firm discipline is really important. I'm exhausted!"

Boy, could I identify with Ginny! For years I felt like the strictest mom in town. In the early years, it seemed like my job was more police sergeant than Mom, and it was discouraging because I saw little success. The children thought I was unfair and often they didn't like me very much. We were in a battle of wills and I wasn't sure I was going to win.

When it comes to discipline, the early years are the most discouraging for parents of young children, primarily because they do not see quick results. And yet these years are the most crucial. John and I have found that the way kids behave in the teen years is determined to a large extent by the first five years of their lives.

A child who does not learn the value of respecting others, their property, or himself may become a teen who gives teachers a bad time, indulges in sexual activity, destroys property for fun, exhibits a poor self-image, and has a weak foundation for his own marriage. As parents we must be very clear about our expectations for behavior and follow through with consistent discipline when we are not obeyed.

Three Key Concepts We Must Teach Our Children

Respect Other People

"You dummy," "You stupid head," and so forth are phrases commonly heard in households with young children. But they must not be permitted. In our household, we explained that these and other demeaning words were not to be spoken. If a child did use these words, we washed the offender's mouth with yucky-tasting soap. It did not take long for the children to get the message.

Verbal abuse of a younger child by an older sibling must not be permitted either. Even if a parent has been too lenient in the child's early years, it is never too late to begin to do what is right. Be honest with your child. Tell him that you have not done things the way you should have and that now changes are going to be made. Certain behavior will no longer be tolerated and specific consequences will follow verbal abuse. But you will have to adhere to the same standards yourself. It will be rough going at first, but persist. The long-range benefits will far outweigh the temporary unpleasantness of clamping down. Personal put-downs have no place in homes where we are striving to build friendships, and Mom and Dad have to follow the same rules.

Sassing parents is another form of verbal abuse children will try. When I was a child, the one thing that made my dad madder than anything else was when one of us kids talked back to Mom. We learned early in life that this was not something we could get away with. Dad's attitude caused us to respect him as well as Mom, and it taught us to respect all those in authority.

Because Dad and Mom never allowed back talk, it never entered my mind to back-talk teachers or other adults. Sassing *any* adult was forbidden territory. Of course, I had arguments with my parents and I disagreed with teachers, but I learned at an early age to treat those in authority with respect.

When we teach our children that every human being is created by God, we instill in them a respect for others. This carries over into appreciating the sacredness of sexuality. Our bodies and our friends' bodies are sacred temples of the Holy Spirit. We must take care not to misuse ourselves or others in any way that God has not designed. God has designed us for sexual fulfillment in marriage only. It is too precious to be shared in any other setting. Respect is the basis for purity.

Respect Each Other's Property

When the twins were small, they were bundles of destruction. They considered anything in their path fair game. It was difficult for the three older children to protect their toys from complete obliteration by two feisty sisters. In an effort to control the damage, we put hooks on each bedroom door just out of the twins' reach and kept the doors locked. As they got bigger, we used other means of discipline. The message was "You must learn to respect other people's property."

When the boys began to mow lawns for pocket money, we invested in a mower and then turned it over to them to maintain. They had to assume the costs of any repair and pay for gas and oil. When they realized it was going to cost them their hard-earned money if they didn't take proper care of the equipment, they learned to respect property.

The women in our family are all about the same size, so it's convenient to borrow clothes from each other. However, the rule is that the clothes must be returned to the owner clean and in top condition and not dumped on the laundry room floor.

We must respect family members' need for privacy. Knock before entering a child's room. Open only mail addressed to you. Regard another as more important than yourself.

Respect Each Other's Word

Prolific western writer Louis L'Amour talks of the "honor" of the Old West. In frontier days, a man's word was the ultimate authority. A bill of sale was rarely made; a written agreement usually wasn't needed. A man's word was enough. *Yes* was *yes* and *no* was *no*. What respect for honesty!

I asked my friend Mary Shannon, who is 22, why she respects her father. She quickly replied, "His integrity. I can count on him, and I know that he means what he says."

Respect must be taught, but it must also be earned. When we continually let down our mates or our children, they will subtly learn that they can't count on us. Perhaps we are always late. We say we'll be on time for our child's game, but we miss the first quarter. When this happens again and again, our child learns he can't depend on us—that we won't do what we say. It would be far better to say we will be late, but we will get there as soon as possible.

When we have clear standards of behavior in our homes and we follow through with necessary discipline to reinforce the behavior, we will encourage the growth of respect.

Cultivate Thoughtfulness

Recently, I hosted the High School Student Government Retreat at our farm. Twenty students descended on the cottage for a day of planning for the new school year. A cookout, games, and lots of paperwork made an understandable mess. As the day drew to a close, my 17-year-old son approached me and asked, "Mom, what can we all do to help clean up?" And then he proceeded to organize the kids into clean-up teams.

His asking wasn't a big deal to him—he probably doesn't even remember doing it—but it was a *big* deal to me. Why? *He* thought of it and *he* suggested it. I had a flashback to those early years of training kids and feeling like I was getting nowhere, of wondering if they would ever stop complaining about chores, of doubting if they would ever initiate a thoughtful action on their own. *Thanks, Lord*, I silently said. *They do eventually learn, even when we feel like failures and want to quit training them.*

Thoughtfulness encourages and demonstrates respect. Chores and manners are invaluable tools in developing thoughtfulness. Each family member should have chores for which he is responsible. A four-year-old child can make his own bed. It might not look exactly the way you want it to, but he's learning responsibility. Praising him reinforces his efforts and builds his self-esteem.

We have a family dish and chore chart. The kids compose it on the computer and post it on the refrigerator. Dad's specialty is bathrooms, but we rotate chores each weekend so no one has to do the same thing all the time. Family members are permitted to trade tasks with one another. What are we trying to teach? Responsibility. Thoughtfulness. How to take care of themselves. I can't clean the whole house by myself. I need the family's help. And I want my boys to learn how to be thoughtful of their wives in the future.

Manners provide us with another means to teach respect. Good manners mean boys stand up when a lady enters the room. They pull out her chair at the table. (My boys practice on their sisters and me.) Good manners mean children call an adult by "Mr." or "Mrs." unless that person tells them it's all right to do otherwise. Good manners means walking a guest to the door when he leaves. These are just a few of the manners we are teaching at our house.

Parents must have the same standards for their behavior as they do for their children's. If we want our kids to respect us, then we need to respect our parents, and our children need to see us doing so. Do I honor my own parents? What about my in-laws? If I am always criticizing them, then my children will grow up to criticize me. When they hear me complain about my parents behind their backs, they will quickly learn to gripe about me behind my back. No one's parents are perfect, and we must choose to honor them in whatever ways we can.

Maximize Teachable Moments

Jerry was taking a walk with his children when they passed a hunched-over, gray-haired old man. The children began to giggle and to make fun of the old man. Seizing the moment, Jerry said, "Kids, don't you know that this man is someone special? The Bible says, 'Gray hair is a crown of splendor; it is attained by a righteous life' (Prov. 16:31). Because of his life experiences, that old man probably has more wisdom than the three of us combined. We mustn't laugh at the elderly, but honor them."

Jerry used a teachable moment to instill in his children a respect for older people. Many teachable moments are present in each day. We must learn to recognize and capitalize on them.

Teachable moments often come when we are sitting at the dinner table or riding in the car. A friend was engaged to be married, and as we sat at the supper table, we discussed the upcoming wedding. One thing led to another and we found ourselves in a lively discussion with our children about what makes a strong marriage. The outcome of the conversation was that everyone agreed that tops on the list was respect. John and I have seen too many marriages begin to unravel when one mate loses respect for the other.

So we said to our kids, "When you begin to date seriously, ask yourself this question, 'Do I respect this person? Why? What do I admire about him or her?'" A simple dinner table conversation provided a natural teachable moment to discuss important issues about marriage.

Ask Their Advice

A different aspect of cultivating respect comes in those moments when we ask our children's advice: I often ask my girls' help in planning a special meal; the other kids frequently edit my writing, and they correct my spelling with great glee. When we ask our children's opinions, we are saying, "I respect your judgment."

Sending children to each other for advice cultivates respect between them. Chris calls his older brother at college for ideas about an essay. The twins ask Chris what classes he thinks they should take in high school. As parents, one of our goals is to encourage our children to go to each other instead of coming to us. They will not always have us, but it is quite likely they will have each other, and fostering mutual respect in the family strengthens those bonds of friendship.

When There's a Family Member You Don't Respect

A friend of mine has a stepfather who is very difficult. He's critical, sarcastic, and self-centered. He drinks too much and has a violent temper. There's really not much in him that she respects.

"How do you respect someone you don't respect?" I asked her.

She commented that it was not easy, but that it had been helpful for her to ask God to show her why her stepdad was the way he was. What was his home life like when he was growing up? Did he have a difficult childhood himself? As she began to discover pieces of his past, her anger was softened by compassion.

She has also chosen to focus on one good thing about him. He is generous. When he comes to visit, he takes the whole family out to dinner, and he buys lovely birthday gifts for her children. It's the only way he knows how to show any kind of care. Realizing that God in His sovereignty has allowed this man to be her stepfather causes my friend to turn her eyes back to God and ask the question, "Lord, what would You like to teach me in this painful relationship that will help me grow?"

It could be that God will use the difficult family member as His instrument to mature us and bless us in ways we cannot imagine. God will use anyone or anything for *good* if we allow Him.

Remember, Nobody's Perfect

It's almost scary to pick up a newspaper or magazine today because there might be a story of a respected Christian leader who has filed for divorce, been caught embezzling funds, or succumbed to some immoral act. Where are the role models for our families? There seem to be very few.

The problem is not new. In Abraham's time, immorality was so rampant that God could not find one moral person in both towns of Sodom and Gomorrah. Ultimately, He destroyed the cities, saving only Lot—Abraham's nephew—and his two daughters. People in Jesus' day had the same problem. Jesus Himself blasted the Pharisees for not practicing what they preached.

While we must respect one another, we must avoid putting anyone on a pedestal. Man is very weak, and when he becomes the object of hero worship, he can become isolated and more susceptible to temptation.

Instead of encouraging hero worship of one or two individuals in society, seek to point out godly character traits that many different individuals possess and lift them up as qualities to be admired and emulated. A young friend might be very shy, yet have an unusual gift of generosity. An older woman may appear stern and unfriendly, yet possess great wisdom. A peer may lack social or intellectual skills, yet be a person of rare integrity. Your husband may be a man of great patience, or your wife may possess unusual compassion. Notice these traits and comment on them. When you point out something to your children that you respect in your mate, you are not only enhancing their respect for that parent, you are also strengthening the marriage friendship.

Ultimately, only God is worthy of complete respect. "The fear (or respect) of the Lord is the beginning of wisdom" (Ps. 111:10, parentheses added). He alone will not let us down. Only His reputation is above repute. In the end, our confidence must be in Him alone.

Choosing what and whom to respect, and becoming people who are worthy of respect, takes time. But as we grow in respect for one another, our friendships within our families will become deeper.

Focus Questions

Meditate on 1 Thessalonians 5:12-24.

1. According to these verses, who are we to respect and how are we to do it?
2. What other actions are mentioned here that will help us cultivate mutual respect among those in our families?
3. Verse 24 is a wonderful promise to memorize. Who is the one who will bring about respect in our families?

Family Friendship Builder

Have a family discussion and talk about character traits that your family members want to develop. What people in history have embodied these traits? Who do you know who has these character traits?

Then, make a list of things you respect in your parents, your grandparents, your in-laws, and your mate. Ask your children what they respect in each older family member.

CHAPTER 6

Celebration: The Daily Joy of Family Friendships

The Lord is my strength and my shield;
My heart trusts in him, and I am helped.
My heart leaps for joy,
And I will give thanks to him in song.

Psalm 28:7

I remember what it was like when I was a teenager and was returning home after being out of town. As the car got closer to the house, my excitement would begin to build. Eagerly, I willed the car to go faster. *Hurry, hurry!* my emotions seemed to say. I couldn't wait to pull into the driveway, honk the horn, and watch the family race out the front door to greet me. I could see the huge smile on Mom's face and the shine of Dad's bald head and his grin spreading from ear to ear.

My mom's and dad's warm embraces, my brothers' and sister's hugs, and everyone's talking at once gave me a thrill and a strong message: "You are special. We love you and we're so glad you're home." Coming home was always a celebration.

It wasn't just me who was greeted this way. It was family friends and any family member who came home. I don't know if Mom and Dad consciously planned the driveway welcoming time or whether it just happened. But whenever my grandparents were due to arrive, one of us kids was posted as a lookout, and the minute the car was spotted, the yell would go out, "They're here! They're here!" and we'd all tumble out the door to greet them.

I am still overwhelmed with those childhood feelings of anticipation as I pull into the driveway of my parents' home with my own kids and honk the horn. I know Mom is waiting to rush out the door with joyful hugs. It's hard, though, because Dad isn't there. He's in heaven and, oh, how I miss him! So now when I go home, I'm overwhelmed with tears—tears of sadness and tears of gratefulness. My mind is flooded with flashbacks of all the times he was there to greet me. In my mind's eye, I can still see him clearly. I can almost feel his big arms around me, and I remember his steadfast love for me.

Now I imagine him in heaven just waiting for me to join him so that he can give me a big hug. His greetings were always so great. I didn't appreciate them at the time. I just took them for granted. Now I know—they were a celebration.

The greeting.

Such a simple thing and yet what a significant impact it can have on others. The Apostle Paul understood the significance of greetings. He took time at the beginning of each of his letters to give a specific greeting to his friends. It always included a reminder of Christ's love and peace. Sometimes the greeting was of a personal nature, and inevitably it reassured his friends about his love and commitment to them.

Come Celebrate

When we think of celebrations in family life, the first things that come to mind are milestone events: birthdays, anniversaries, and graduations. Certainly, these are significant times of celebration. However, in the daily routine of family life there are *many* simple things we can celebrate.

We seem to have lost the art of celebration. We are tempted to think we're too busy, it's too much trouble, and occasionally, *It doesn't make that much difference anyway. No one seems to care and the family doesn't seem to appreciate it. So why bother?* Perhaps we're barely getting done what needs doing and the thought of more things to do, like planning a celebration, is overwhelming. Is celebrating really that important anyway?

Yes, it is!

Life today is difficult. Problems challenge us and we worry about our children's futures. It's easy to fall into the trap of taking ourselves too seriously, of worrying about success, jobs, acceptance, parenting, illnesses, and so on. It's easy to lose our ability to laugh. It's easy to forget the simple ways of purely enjoying one another. Celebration keeps us balanced in a difficult world, renews our perspective, and enables us to recapture joy. It provides us with an easy means of building friendships within the family. A real benefit of celebration is that it can be very simple and yet the dividends are so great. Here are some ideas for celebration that will encourage us to recapture joy in our homes.

Four Simple Things to Celebrate

The Greeting

We have a golden retriever named Duchess. She's a great dog and she loves me. Whenever I come home, she hears my footsteps on the front porch and comes to meet me. As I open the door, she greets me with her tail wagging so hard her whole body sways. Often she'll race around trying to find something to hold in her mouth (her retriever instinct) and she'll bring it to me as a gift while howling in the process. She makes coming home fun because she's excited to see me.

Lately though, Duchess has slowed down. Having raised five kids and approaching the age of 12, she deserves a rest. In the hot summer months, she curls up on the cool basement floor and doesn't always come to greet me with enthusiasm. In fact, she often sleeps through my return. I feel a little empty when I open the door and she's not there. I miss her warm greeting.

Sometimes when my family comes in, I act a lot more like Duchess does in her old age than like she did earlier in her life. It's so much easier to keep on doing what I'm doing than to go to the front door and greet the kids or John with hugs as they arrive home at the end of the day. After all, they already know I love them. So, do I really need to stop and go greet them? Yes! It's only a *little* celebration, but it makes such a *big* difference. Giving John a warm embrace reminds him that I love him and reminds the kids of the security of our marriage relationship. His hug and greeting illustrate for our sons the importance of cherishing the wives God will one day give them. When I greet my children, I remind them that they are special to me.

Recently, we took our church staff away for a couple of days of refreshment and relaxation. Several of the staff came the second day. When it was time for them to arrive, John led us all outside to greet the newcomers and to carry in their bags. As their cars pulled up, we cheered. And as each staff member got out of the car, we greeted him or her with enthusiasm. Hugging one woman, I said, "I'm so glad you're here." With tears in her eyes, she remarked, "I've never had a greeting like this before." This simple celebration set the tone for the entire retreat.

A simple greeting can become a genuine celebration that says to family members and friends, "You're special. I'm glad that you are my friend."

Mealtimes

"Grab it, zap it, eat it, and run" has become the way we view mealtime in our busy households. It's often hard to find a time when the whole family can sit down to a meal together. Eating together may involve some tough choices, but mealtimes can be simple events of great celebration.

Preparing food, eating, and cleaning up together provide opportunities for family team building. Kids talk in a relaxed manner as two of them chop carrots for a salad. An older brother gets better acquainted with a younger sister as they do dishes together.

My friend Marilyn is a musician. She traces part of her love for music back to the time when kids in her family did dishes together. Her mom played music and they sang together as they worked. My kids groan if I sing, but Marilyn's mom found a great way for their family to have fun doing dishes, and Marilyn became a musician.

In our home, we try to eat breakfast together. Fifteen minutes may be all we have before the kids race for the school bus, but breakfast is our way to begin the day together. Each person shares something he has going on that day. Susy has a math quiz, Chris a student council meeting, and Dad a difficult counseling situation. We take a few minutes to pray for each other's day. Then we head out the door. Dinnertime gives us a chance to report on how our day went.

Occasionally, we'll prepare a special dessert for dinner. When the children were small, we colored paper place mats or decorated napkins. Sometimes we have a "question of the meal," such as "What would you do if you were president?" or "What would you do with one million dollars?" Thought-provoking questions like these enable us to get to know each other a bit better.

Turning the television off, taking the phone off the hook (or putting the answering machine on), and sitting at a table facing each other all help make family meals a special occasion—a celebration—instead of a place where short-order meals are gobbled down. And the relaxed communication that takes place provides relationships with one more opportunity to grow.

Communication takes work, and in our entertainment-oriented society, it's easier to be entertained than it is to communicate. In celebrating meals together, we take the time to sharpen our communication skills. This enables us to forge deeper friendships with one another.

New Seasons

A change in seasons offers us a convenient time to celebrate. A picnic in spring, the first swim in summer, a walk through the leaves in fall, or the first snowman in winter can become simple opportunities to create special celebrations.

We lived in Pennsylvania when the children were small, and each year in late fall, we eagerly awaited the few days of Indian summer the area would have. First, several cold days would signal the approaching winter. Then, the sun would suddenly burst forth with an unexpectedly warm day as if it couldn't quite bear to leave summer behind. This type of gorgeous day was perfect for our last picnic of the year!

The children and I would grab an old blanket, pick John up at the office, go to McDonald's to get our food, and head to our favorite tree in Edgeworth Park for lunch. It was always an inconvenient time for Dad. To begin with, he was usually in a bad mood. He felt he had no business playing hooky from a demanding job for a picnic. But he succumbed to family pressure, and we laughingly named this picnic "Dad's Grumpy Picnic." It became a kind of humorous tradition. Each fall we found ourselves waiting for the perfect day and reminding Dad to prepare to be grumpy! Now when we go back to visit in Pennsylvania, we always go by "our tree" and retell the stories of those celebrations and the fun they turned out to be.

New seasons of life are also opportunities to celebrate. When your teenage son finally needs to shave, encourage Dad to take him to the store for his first razor and then out for dessert to celebrate man to man. It can be traumatic when your daughter has her first menstrual period. Slip a bouquet of flowers quietly into her room with a note that says,

"Congratulations on becoming a woman. We are so proud of you and of the beautiful lady you are. God has special plans for you, and we are so thankful and honored to be your parents."

Look for small ways to make new seasons of life a cause for celebration.

The Nonreason

Life is serious and sometimes there doesn't seem to be much reason to celebrate. But we still can. Celebrating can provide a great pick-me-up and help to restore perspective.

Our car used to have incredible urges for ice cream. We would be in the middle of dinner when an attack might occur. John was usually the one who heard the groans. All of a sudden he'd say, "Listen! I hear it! It's getting louder and louder. The car's having an ice cream attack! I guess we'd better get in it quickly!" We'd all pile into the car and watch John pretend to try to control it as we made our way toward the nearest ice cream shop.

Sometimes we'd already be in the car and perhaps even caught in the middle of a traffic jam when an attack would occur. "Uh-oh!" My husband would cry out. "It's happening! I can't control the car! It wants to go to the ice cream shop." And he would pretend to have a battle with the steering wheel—but the car always won and we always got ice cream.

My friend's boys discovered a vacant old shed that had a cement slab porch. One summer evening, Anne and her husband, Todd, were near the shed collecting fireflies with the boys. "Hey!" one said. "This would make a great dance floor."

With that, Anne and Todd began to sing as their young boys started dancing, jumping, and yelling together. The old shed was soon dubbed "The Dancing House," and many times one of the boys would say, "Hey, let's go down to The Dancing House!"

Celebrating for no reason is merely taking time to create special memories together. One of our favorite nonreason celebrations is to set up empty plastic bottles in a bowling pin formation. Then we get down on our knees with a tennis ball and see how many bottles we can knock down. Children, young and old, enjoy this game, and it's sure to produce laughter and cries of, "Please, just one more time, Mom!"

I have found it was easier to take time to celebrate for no reason when my children were small than it has been as they've grown older. It's so easy for each of us to get involved in doing our own thing and neglect celebrating *together*. Yet, even if you've never begun traditions and celebrated together, it's not too late. If you lack ideas, brainstorm with some other parents. It's fun and encouraging to try their ideas and then report back to them how your celebration went. Don't be discouraged if an idea falls flat. Just maintain a sense of humor and try another!

Significant Events to Celebrate

Birthdays

Birthdays are probably the most regularly celebrated family event. Yet they can be the source of great disappointment. Perhaps you grew up in a home where birthdays were a big deal, but in your husband's family, they were not. Each year when your birthday approaches, your expectations rise. But he forgets or makes a last-minute effort to get a gift or buy a cake. Then, the gift he gets you is a new frying pan you needed, but not the bracelet you secretly hoped for. Now you feel hurt, bitter, unloved, and unappreciated. Year after year we are disappointed because we approach birthdays with different expectations—expectations that have been shaped, in part, by the homes in which we grew up.

Much pain can be avoided if we recognize our differing expectations and talk together about how we want to celebrate birthdays within our own family. Each family will celebrate differently. There are two extremes that we should avoid: overdoing it and barely doing it.

In some instances, birthday celebrations can become a subtle form of competition between adults. It becomes a matter of which family can have the best party for their children, which party costs the most, and which is the most unique. In one community, a birthday party for a fourth grader involved renting rooms at a nearby luxury hotel for an overnight slumber party. In another neighborhood, the mother of a six-year-old reserved the ballroom of the country club for her daughter's catered party. Adult competition can subtly replace the real reason for the celebration—to give thanks for, and to honor, the person. And we can find ourselves with a serious case of overdoing it.

Good intentions can also get us into trouble. My sister, Fran, tells the story of the year she had three birthday parties for her daughter, who was turning eight. My sister was feeling sad for this middle child, who had come through a rough year. She determined to make her birthday special. First she had a family party, then another party with 15 little girls, and a third at Grandmother's house with more extended family and gifts. After the third party, the exhausted child burst into tears and said, "Mom, please don't do this again." It had just been too much.

My Canadian friends with 11 children had simple, yet meaningful, birthday traditions. Early in the morning, the family served the birthday person tea and sweets in bed. Each child had his own special china teacup used only on birthdays. The birthday person did not have to do chores on his birthday, and he was treated like royalty for the entire day.

When the birthday child came to breakfast, his chair was decorated all over with festive balloons and paper. And if the birthday child was small, he would find a tiny chair on top of the table where he was allowed to eat breakfast presiding over the family. Each family member made, rather than bought, a card for the birthday person. Elna, a member of that family who is now grown, still has a box of homemade birthday cards from all her birthdays. Those cards are among her greatest treasures.

Some of us may feel we're too busy to celebrate or write a note to honor another. The best we may manage is to say "happy birthday" and give an unwrapped gift picked up on the way home.

One friend whose tendency is to barely do birthdays is the mother of sons. However, she has begun to make a big deal out of birthdays—not only theirs, but hers as well. She has helped her husband and sons learn how to pamper her on her birthday. My husband asked her why she had begun to do this if birthdays didn't matter that much to her. She responded, "I'm training my sons how to pamper their future wives. Their wives may have greater expectations for birthdays than I do. I want my sons to be thoughtful, loving husbands."

Here are some ideas for making birthdays significant without going to great expense:

- I have a friend who sews. She has made a flag for each family member. She appliqués on the flag the family member's name and likenesses of things he likes. The flag flies on the pole by the front door on the birthday person's special day.
- Another friend tapes paper banners to her front door that read, "Happy birthday___. We love you!"
- One husband cooks dinner for his wife. She isn't allowed in the kitchen on her birthday until her feast is ready.
- In another family, each person takes a turn telling the honoree something that they love about him such as, "I love the way you help me with my math and don't get mad when I don't get it."

In your family you can enlist a child to help think up new ideas for honoring the birthday person. This spreads the fun and encourages creative celebrating.

Holidays

Valentine's Day has always been fun in our family. A couple of weeks before February 14, we draw names for secret valentine pals. Over the next several days, we do special things for that person. It might be a love note in disguised handwriting left on a pillow, candy smuggled with the help of a friend into a school locker, or chores mysteriously done by another. A guessing game ensues as we try to figure out who the secret valentine pal might be. To throw one another off the trail of discovery, we've even done things for someone who wasn't our secret valentine. Once, in an airport, one of the kids had his valentine paged. The excited child was given a note on which was written a silly jingle! On Valentine's Day we have a family dinner and each person reads a poem to his valentine revealing his identity.

Simple? Yes.

Silly? Perhaps.

But positive steps in building relationships? Definitely.

When our children were little, Easter meant church, candy eggs, and playacting. After church we'd head to the farm for our annual reproduction of the Easter morning play. Each family member was assigned a character in the Easter morning story and had to craft a costume out of whatever he could find in half an hour. We then acted out our version of that glorious morning while Dad read the story. An old, faded photo of Allison dressed up as Mary Magdalene in a bright red bathrobe that was way too big for her and a lopsided head wrap is a happy reminder of those early Easter celebrations.

Many books are available that have creative ideas for using holidays to build family relationships. Ann Hibbard's *Family Celebration Series* published by Baker Book House has many suggestions.

Vacations

Vacations are special holidays that naturally lend themselves to celebrations. Blair, Jay, and their two small boys recently took a vacation at home. They canceled all their obligations and events during that time. Free from demanding jobs and the constraints of usually scheduled activities, they now had time to relax. During the day they chased butterflies, collected rocks, and enjoyed God's world together in simple, yet special, celebration. In the evenings, after dinner, they took family walks.

Bob, Elaine, and their three teens went to the seashore for their family vacation. Used to a highly stressful, busy life at home, all they really wanted and needed was time to relax together without other people or distractions. They are all avid readers and so they spent much time curled up with books. In the evenings, they walked down to the pier and watched the incoming fishing boats.

Each family member also took his turn at cooking meals. One day, Rob caught a 10-pound bluefish that he cleaned, baked, and stuffed—albeit with some help from Mom—and proudly served on his night as cook. Celebrating each other quietly together, with no agenda and no extra people, was just what this busy family needed.

Special Accomplishments to Celebrate

Graduation signifies a major accomplishment. It provides a natural opportunity to celebrate. Sarah and Eugenia recently graduated from high school. Their moms wanted to do something to honor them for their accomplishment. They planned a special dinner for their families and a few others who had significantly influenced the two girls.

Before the day of the dinner, the parents collected old pictures of the girls and had them made into slides. During the evening they surprised the guests with a slide show, complete with a selection of carefully chosen music. Much laughter erupted as the girls watched their lives unfold on the screen.

After the slide show each guest took a minute to share with Eugenia and Sarah some way in which each had been a blessing. Sarah's dad talked about her faith and how she had been an encouragement and an example to him as she prayed for him. Eugenia's dad shared how much he had appreciated her and how much he had learned from her ability to stick to things even when they were difficult. After the guests spoke, the girls took a few minutes to tell each person what they meant to them.

It was a beautiful celebration that left the two girls, and everyone else who heard what was said, feeling built up and appreciated. The cost was minimal but the value priceless.

Accomplishments come in different forms. Lauren, our young friend who is severely retarded, recently achieved a major accomplishment. At age nine, after many years of therapy, she finally began to crawl. What a time of celebration followed. Emily, her younger sister, began to clap and sing. "Lauren's crawling! Lauren's crawling! Clap for Lauren!"

The family began to dance and sing together celebrating her major accomplishment. Their mutual joy in Lauren's achievement added another bond to their family friendships.

The Old Testament builder Nehemiah understood the importance of celebrating. After the long, hard work of rebuilding the walls around Jerusalem, bickering among themselves, and fighting the enemy, the Israelites' work was finally finished. Nehemiah and Ezra called for a celebration. So great was their joy, it was said to be the greatest celebration in nearly 150 years (Neh. 8:17). Certainly there would be difficult times ahead, but relationships had been forged, the faith of the people strengthened, and God had been honored for His faithfulness to them. Nehemiah and Ezra knew the value of celebrating.

We must take time to celebrate in our families. A wise man once said, "When we get to heaven, God is going to ask us a question. He is going to say, 'Well, how did you like the world that I made for you? Did you enjoy it? Did you have fun in it?'" I hope we can answer yes.

Focus Questions

Meditate on Nehemiah 8.

1. Using your imagination, describe the scene in this chapter as if you were a reporter for a newsmagazine.
2. What is the relationship between joy and strength (v. 10)? Using a concordance, look up as many other passages as you can find that contain the word *joy*. Write out the one that means the most to you today.
3. What can you do in your family this week to create a spirit of celebration? Plan two *simple* things.

Family Friendship Builder

Working together, make a list of fun things to do as a family. Ask other parents for their creative ideas for family fun. Make sure at least half of the activities involve no extra expense. Let one family member choose and plan an event each month. Set a date for the first event.

CHAPTER 7

Prayer: The Invisible Bond of Family Friendships

*I pray also for those who will believe in me
through their message, that all of them may be one,
Father, just as you are in me and I am in you."*
John 17:20-21

I wanted to be full of joy. Looking around I saw majestic snow-covered peaks in every direction. A clear blue sky reigned over a mountaintop bursting with colorful wildflowers. Only the laughter of the children broke the silence. There was such peace—peace everywhere but inside me. I wasn't peaceful and I wasn't joyful.

We were on Mount Rainier for a family vacation. John and the four younger children were hiking somewhere on the rocky path ahead of me. My thoughts were not with them; they were with Allison, who was lost somewhere in France.

A couple of days earlier, friends in whose home she was to be visiting had called to tell us she had not arrived. She had been traveling in Europe with another girl. They had only a tentative itinerary. Throughout the trip, she had always been reliable and had let her hosts know her plans. But there had been a storm that had temporarily halted phone service, and I tried to believe that our friends had not heard from her because she simply could not reach them. However, my active and motherly imagination had visualized all kinds of possible tragedies. Where was my daughter and was she all right? Several days had passed now with no word, and I was sick of praying and worrying. Plus, I was becoming a real drag to the rest of the family. "Please God," I prayed, "help me to trust You and to leave her in Your hands."

Forcing myself to concentrate on the character of God, I gazed again at the huge, powerful mountains surrounding me. Then I thought about the 35 different varieties of wildflowers we had counted on our walk. How beautifully the mountains illustrated the power of God, while the delicate flowers showed His loving attention to detail.

Surely, I reasoned, *our heavenly Father with His awesome power and gentle concern for the tiniest details will take care of Allison.* Encouraged by this visible reminder of God's power and love, I hurried to catch up with the rest of the family.

Allison called the next day. She was fine. The storm *had* prevented her from contacting our friends by phone. I learned several valuable lessons through this experience. I was reminded that God cares for my child. He wants me to pray for her. He delights when we pray for our children as He has prayed for us. But a deeper lesson for me was learning to relinquish control.

There was nothing I could do for Allison except pray. And I didn't like that because I wanted to be in control. I had to give her into the care of her heavenly Father. He took care of her when I couldn't. And He will continue to care for her and my other children as they become adults and as my control lessens. By praying for my child, I experienced God's gentle, personal touch. His desire is that we, as parents, learn and grow as we pray for our children.

The Significance of Prayer

Prayer is not merely going to God with a shopping list of things we want Him to do for us and for our families. Rather, it is being in relationship with Him, listening to Him, and sharing our hearts with Him.

Oswald Chambers says, "We look upon prayer as a means of getting things for ourselves; the Bible's idea of prayer is that we may get to know

God Himself."[1] We must remember *who* it is that we are talking with—the Almighty God. I have found it helpful to begin and end my prayers by focusing on His character traits. He is the Almighty God. He is the God who heals. He is the God of peace. He is the God who forgives. He is the God who provides, and He is the God who is in control. He knows everything that is happening. He is not caught off guard. His love is perfect.

As I consider *who* He is instead of focusing on myself or another person or my situation, I am better able to pray with faith. When I look at what God has to work with—me, my mate, my child, or my extended family—my expectations can be small, but when I focus on who He is, it is easier to believe.

As we pray, it is important to have a teachable spirit, a heart that is continually open to whatever God might want to show us. Some of His most sacred lessons for us come as we pray for our family members.

Recently my sister-in-law Ginny and I were catching up on family news. As we talked, we discovered that we each had a similar concern for our children—one of hers and one of mine. Neither child had a severe problem, but our mothers' instincts voiced concern. We agreed that we would each pray for both children every day for the next month.

Why pray? We needed help! We can't be everything to our children; only God can. It is an encouragement to have a prayer partner. Often, we need the support of another praying parent.

Prayer is a great privilege and a tremendous responsibility. The Old Testament prophet Samuel said to his people, "As for me, far be it from me that I should sin against the Lord by failing to pray for you" (1 Sam. 12:23). The command to pray cannot be much clearer than this.

One result of praying is that our children will see that their parents need God. When they see us on our knees, when they hear us ask for prayer, and when they pray with us, they are living in the reality that our security and theirs is in God.

Recently, Allison shared with her dad how much it meant to her that he got up early every morning to pray for her. Knowing that he prays regularly gives her a sense of security, and it also illustrates his need for God.

Praying for One Another

It was there, posted in clear sight on the kitchen cabinet, in my husband's barely legible handwriting. The note said:

Family! Be sure to take some time this week to think through and write out your personal needs and goals for the coming year. Thursday night we'll have a family night and share with each other.

Love, Dad

"Oh, no," groaned one of our 14-year-old twins. "Do we have to do this again?" With a heavy sigh of exasperation, she went in search of her twin whom she knew would provide some groaning companionship.

Quietly watching this scene, I couldn't help but smile at her reaction. After all, it's part of a teen's job description to groan at parental suggestions.

When Thursday night rolled around, we gathered around the table with our notebooks to hear from one another. It was a precious time during which each of us took a turn sharing with the others our prayer needs for the coming year.

One twin hoped to have one special friend, yet avoid cliques and be friendly to everyone. The other twin wanted to reach out more to nonbelievers and invite them to Cornerstone, our youth ministry. One child wanted to read at least 30 minutes a day, while another desired not to be such a perfectionist. One of the boys hoped to maintain a better sense of humor. Everyone, it seemed, wanted to have disciplined times of Bible study and better eating habits! My husband wanted to work less and play more, and I needed prayer for the ability to write this book, as my confidence level was anemic.

Most telling, though, was the sheepish confession of our college son, John. "I hate to admit this, but before Dad even posted his note, I had been thinking about my year and typed out my needs and goals on the computer. Here they are."

Thank you, Lord, I thought. *He has graduated from the protest stage and can now realize for himself how helpful this process can be. What a blessing!*

This was not a new idea for our family. We had been goal setting with the children each August for several years. Before they were old enough to join us, John and I would take some time alone to think through our own lives and the lives of our children, focusing on five areas of growth: spiritual, emotional, physical, mental, and social. We discussed and wrote down the needs we observed, and this became our prayer list for each child and for one another during the following year. When the children became old enough, we showed them how to do it for themselves. In addition to the family prayer lists, John and I still have our private parents' prayer list for the kids as well.

Why do we do this? We do it because it helps us to know specifically how to pray for and to encourage one another throughout the year. We get to know each other at a deeper level. Our friendships become stronger and we have a greater sense of being a family team—a team whose head is the Lord. As our kids get older, our roles subtly shift from that of authority figures to peers. Parents and children begin to come to God as equals, praying for one another.

What do we do if our mate is not a believer? Be sensitive to your mate's feelings and beliefs and modify the goal-setting exercise. Under these circumstances, it is still helpful for the family to share needs and goals for the coming year and to encourage one another. This simple goal-setting technique is not unlike what is done in a business setting. And you can still pray for what the others share.

This is just one way to pray for each other in our families; there are many others. Both John and I have a list of character traits that we are praying our children develop—traits such as the ability to fail and cope with failure, to be a person of integrity, to forgive others, and to ask forgiveness.[2] Occasionally, I will take some of the great prayers in the Scriptures and insert one of my children's names there.

Paul's letter to the Ephesians is an example: "I keep asking that the God of our Lord Jesus Christ, the glorious Father, may give (insert person's name) the Spirit of wisdom and revelation so that (name) may know him better. I pray also that the eyes of (name's) heart may be enlightened in order that he/she may know the hope to which He has called (name), the riches of his glorious inheritance in the saints, and his incomparable great power for (name) who believe" (see Eph. 1:17-19).

Praying Generationally

On a recent church staff retreat we asked the question, "Who in your background has influenced your coming to faith in Christ?" It was amazing to see that the majority of those attending had been influenced by the prayers of a great-grandparent, great-aunt, or someone else from a previous generation.

In speaking of God's covenant, Isaiah says, "'My spirit, who is on you, and my words that I have put in your mouth will not depart from your mouth, or from the mouth of your children, or from the mouths of their descendants from this time on and forever,' says the Lord" (Isa. 59:21). Our God is a God of generations, and over and over again in His Word we see His concern for the generations to come.

A small child can put his hands on his mother's swollen tummy and pray for the child she is carrying. Another child can pray for God's special choice of a sibling to be adopted. An aunt who is a single woman can pray for her niece who is struggling in her faith. Because of her unique position, God may give her a significant ministry in this child's life.

Ever since our children were tiny, we have prayed for their future mates. Allison gave her sisters a beautiful poster depicting a small girl walking along a path holding the hand of a young boy. "This represents your future husband," she said. "Begin to pray for him now."

Once when she was small, I overheard Susy praying, "Dear God, please bless the boy I am going to marry and help his parents to be raising him right!" I hope children somewhere are praying that for us!

God will not call all of us to marry. Marriage is not a higher calling. Some are *called* to the single life, and there are many benefits to being single. But everyone, single or married, can impact generations to come as they pray.

Finding Time to Pray

I really didn't want to get up early. I'm not a morning person, but the day ahead was packed and I knew I needed some time alone with God. So more out of determination than desire, I dragged myself out of bed, put the kettle on for some coffee, and curled up for a time of prayer and Bible study.

Setting aside a regular time and place for personal quiet time with God has been both the hardest and the most important discipline in my life. I'm not always faithful. Many days I miss, but when I spend time alone with God I am always encouraged.

We each need a special time alone with our heavenly Father—a time in which we pray specifically for our family and friends and about our schedule for the day. Reading a chapter from the Psalms and the Book of Proverbs inspires my time alone. When I take more time to study the Scriptures, my faith is deepened. It's amazing to consider that a holy God desires my fellowship. He wants to be with me, and it brings Him great joy when I take time to be alone with Him.

Setting aside time for a personal reflection is the first step in an effective prayer life. Mealtime and bedtime are other natural times to pray with family members.

We have a bulletin board by our breakfast table that highlights photos of friends who live out of town. Usually, they are Christmas cards. Each morning at breakfast a different family member picks a photo and we pray for those in the picture.

"Flashing-sign times" are special times throughout the day that I try to remember to pray.

Driving alone in the car used to be a flashing-sign time for me. That is, until I forgot to keep my eyes open and rear-ended someone in the middle of rush hour on the Washington beltway. On another occasion, while praying in the car, I forgot how fast I was going and got a speeding ticket. Finally, John said, "Susan, please don't pray anymore when you are driving the car!"

So I've designated some other flashing-sign times. When I see a school bus, I pray for the kids on that bus and those at the school my children attend. When we hear a siren, the children and I pray for whoever is involved. If I'm in the school parking lot waiting for kids, I pray for the students and faculty. My husband prays in the shower. A friend prays when he mows grass. Another prays when she vacuums. Flashing-sign times serve as a simple reminder to me to pray.

"Needy times" are another natural time to pray. Once a college student stopped by our house on his way to a job interview. He was nervous, so we took a few minutes to pray for his interview. Another time, a young friend was deeply hurt because some kids in the neighborhood had mistreated him. It was a natural time to put my arms around him and pray for him to be comforted and for the other kids to learn to be kind and not exclusive. It's easy to think, *I'll pray about that later.* And then later comes and we forget. I've found it is better to pray when the need arises.

Asking forgiveness is another example of prayer in a time of need. It's all too easy to harbor a feeling of resentment toward our mate or a bad attitude toward a difficult child. Instead, I must go to God right away, confess my bad attitude, and ask Him to forgive me and change my heart. And, if it's appropriate, I should go to the person and ask forgiveness as well. The most important ingredient in family life is that of forgiveness.

Enlisting Others to Pray

At nearly 87 years of age, my mother-in-law is not as physically strong as she used to be, but her spirit is stronger than ever. Early in the morning you will find her on her knees praying for her children and grandchildren. She has a coverlet on which is cross-stitched the names of each of her 15 grandchildren, and she prays for them every day.

In the evening before she crawls into bed, she is once again on her knees praying for her family. Occasionally, she awakens in the night with a specific burden for someone. Again, she crawls out of bed and slips to her knees to intercede for her loved ones. What an example she is! And how God has used her faithfulness in our lives!

Grandparents can have a special ministry of prayer. But what if you don't have any grandparents? Adopt some. There are many older saints who would be thrilled to be adopted as grandparents to pray for and to encourage you and your family. And if you don't have any biological children of your own, adopt some and pray for them. We can have many spiritual children through prayer.

In our Episcopal denomination, we have godparents. A godparent is someone chosen by the parents to be a special prayer partner and encourager for a new baby. Throughout the child's life, this person prays for him and acts as a spiritual adviser. It's a wonderful tradition. I try to let the godparents of my children know specific things for which my child needs prayer. These godparents provide a wonderful support for us. It is a blessing to know someone else is praying for our child.

If your denomination doesn't have godparents, create them. Consider asking a single person to be the godparent of your child. Have him come for dinner. Spend time with him, and as your child grows, provide the two of them with opportunities to be together to develop a relationship.

Every month I meet with four women. One is a grandmother and one is a new mother. Our life experiences and ages are very different, but we share an unusual bond. Our purpose in meeting is simply to share personal needs and pray for one another. Between our meetings we call each other when we have a prayer concern. This covenant group has been a tremendous support to me.

I meet with a different group of women on a weekly basis. We are all about the same age and our children are close in age. Our purpose is specific. We meet to pray for the public schools that our children attend. For nearly nine years we have been praying for the students, faculty, staff, and school board. We have seen God do many miracles in our kids' lives and in our own lives as well.

Praying with others strengthens us. It gives us a sense of accountability for our lives, and it provides a living example to the rest of the world of a little church.

The Scriptures and Prayer

A couple of days after my dad died unexpectedly, I flew home from the funeral to a speaking engagement. I was feeling very sad, and the last thing I wanted to do was speak. But I had made a commitment and I had a sense that it was something I should keep. So I got dressed, asked the family to pray especially hard for me, and went off to speak. When I returned home this is what I found on my pillow:

> *Dear Mommy,*
>
> *How was your talk? Did it go well? We sure hope so. We prayed real hard for you. Here are a few verses to cheer ya up. Sleep real well.*
>
> *Love,*
> *The twins*

Accompanying this note was a Bible with several strips of torn notebook paper inserted with these verse references written on them: John 8:51, Isa. 26:19, Ps. 16:8-11, 17:15, 49:15, and 73:23-26.

Looking up the verses in the Bible, I was comforted. But even better, my heart was filled to overflowing at the underlying message my girls gave me. *They* knew where to go for comfort—God's Word. Somehow, over the years, they had learned that in His Word we find true comfort. How I thanked God for revealing this to them and for using them to encourage me!

Being familiar with God's Word and talking to Him in prayer go hand in hand. In His Word we come to know His heart. We observe examples of answered prayer. Sometimes God answers our prayers *yes*, sometimes *no*, and occasionally He says to *wait*. Often with the wait there is silence. Silence is hard to understand; but God always answers out of His great love for us, much as we answer our children's requests. Sometimes, for our children's own good and because we love them, we must say no.[3] Isaiah tells us that God's thoughts are not our thoughts; neither are His ways our ways, but as the heavens are higher than the earth, so are His ways higher than our ways and His thoughts higher than our thoughts (see Isa. 55:8, 9). Nor is God limited by our timetable. He is not in a hurry. He has an eternity to develop us and our children. Above all, He is a good God who delights in us and in our children.

As we continue to grow in prayer, it is helpful to remember these final thoughts:

- God specifically, carefully, and lovingly chose each member of my family.
- He is a loving God who desires good for each of us.
- He is in control.
- He loves my children, my marriage partner, and others in my family even more than I do.

Focus Questions

Meditate on John 17.

1. What different groups of people does Jesus pray for?
2. List the specific things He prays for those He loves.
3. Put a family member's name beside each thing you listed in number two and pray this for them. Don't forget to include yourself.

Family Friendship Builder

Make a list of qualities that you would like God to develop in your life and in the lives of your children, grandchildren, godchildren, nieces, and nephews. Pick one day each week that you will pray for a particular child.

PART THREE

Cultivating Our Closest Friendships

CHAPTER 8

Friendship Between Husband and Wife

Submit to one another out of reverence for Christ.
Ephesians 5:21

It has been a couple of weeks, I thought as I considered how long I'd been feeling indifferent toward my husband, John. Curled up by a roaring fire, I was trying to have a quiet time. I had some writing that I should have been doing, but in my heart I knew that what I really needed was a good, long, honest talk with God and no one else.

At that particular moment, dissatisfaction and irritation would have best described my attitude toward my husband. There wasn't any one thing that made me feel this way. We hadn't fought. I knew of no unresolved issue between us and he probably wasn't even aware of how I was feeling. If he had noticed my distance, he had probably assumed it was hormones, worry about the kids, or my busy schedule.

But I knew that when my thoughts turned to John, they weren't pleasant. Instead, I found myself thinking, *He's not been very affectionate lately. How can he expect me to feel romantic toward him when he hasn't made an effort to really talk to me and to give me hugs? He's almost always consumed by his work. I wish he'd ask me what I am really thinking about. I wonder if he cares that I get tired of all the carpooling, cooking, cleaning, and working. And the two things I asked him to do last week, he still hasn't done. When I told him something I thought he needed to do at the office, it just irritated him. I was only trying to help. And I wish he'd help the kids with their homework for a change.* The more I thought about him, the more dissatisfied I became.

This is great, I mused. *We've been married more than 24 years. We do have a good marriage. We speak and write about marriage and the family. We are the model couple to many people, but at this moment I don't really like my husband.*

As I sat by the glowing embers of the dying fire and struggled with my thoughts, I prayed, *God, please help me. Show me what's not right in my life. Help me to like my husband. Please change me.*

We could be called the generation of great expectations. We want to be everything we can be, have everything we need, have people like us, and experience complete fulfillment. In addition, we sincerely want to raise children who love God, one another, and us. We want happy marriages, and we want it all *now*. At the same time, we are overwhelmed by the stresses of providing for our families, dual careers, and children's needs. Then, there's church involvement, volunteer commitments, extended family crises, and social obligations.

No wonder our marriages sometimes get put on the back burner until life calms down. After all, we reason, we have a pretty good relationship, and right now building a strong friendship with my budding teenager is more important than working on my marriage. By the time I've helped two daughters learn how to get along with each other, my relationship-building tank is drained. I'm too exhausted to put any energy into my marriage. It can wait.

But it can't!

I believe that next to our relationship with God, our relationship with our mate is the most important one of all. A solid marriage friendship sets the tone for building other healthy relationships within the family.

Many of us are child-oriented. It's easier to focus on our relationships with our children than on our marriage. When a child is going through a particularly difficult stage, it's easy to put all of our emotional energy into helping him work through this stressful time. If we are the parents of an only child, it is even easier to find our lives totally revolving around him. If we are dissatisfied in the marriage relationship, instead of dealing with our problem, we put all of our energy into building our relationship with our children. We begin to look to them to meet emotional needs that we should be looking to our mates to meet.

In the long run, each of these tendencies to be child-oriented does a great disservice to our children. It puts unfair pressure on them while permitting us to neglect the cultivation of our marriage. We have our children for only approximately 18 years, but we have our mates for many more than that. Many marriages fall apart when the last child leaves home because all of the parents' energy went into raising the children. The couple then finds they have little in common with each other.

Do we want our children to have strong marriages? If we do, then they need to see us taking time to cultivate our own marriages. Strong marriage friendships don't just happen. They take work. And as our children see us working on ours, they will have a realistic picture for their own marriages.

In seeking to build a strong marriage friendship, there are three traps to avoid and three gems to polish.

Three Traps to Avoid in a Marriage Friendship

The Picky Trap

I came to several realizations that chilly day when I sat before the fire and struggled with my thoughts. What if John gave me the attention I wanted, did what I asked him to do, and spent time with the kids the way I thought he should? Then what? In all honesty, I realized I would probably think of something else that was dissatisfying me or that I felt needed improvement. I had fallen into the trap of being a picky wife. And picky people don't encourage strong friendships. They can never be pleased. Their focus is on "if only you had or hadn't" or "if only you would or wouldn't." Picky people always want something more.

What causes us to be so picky? Could it be that our expectations are unrealistic? We act as if there is a perfect mate, and when we realize ours isn't, we set about to make them perfect—or at least to improve them.

Of course, serious problems in a marriage relationship should not be overlooked or denied. A couple may need good counseling to resolve the issues. If there are serious problems, it's helpful to ask, "Am I falling into the picky trap, or is this a serious issue that needs to be dealt with?"

The Comparison Trap

One morning over coffee at a weekly study group, my friend dropped a bomb. "I'm so frustrated with my husband," she announced. "I hate his measly job. I look at my friends who are married to lawyers with exciting careers, and I'm embarrassed by what my husband does. I'm thinking of leaving him."

There was a stunned silence in the room as we took in what she had said. She and her husband were people of deep faith. They had several children and a lovely home. But as she looked at those around her whose lives seemed more exciting, she became dissatisfied with her own. The more she thought about it, the more miserable she became. She had fallen into the comparison trap.

Fortunately, my friend was an open-minded person, and as our small group challenged her, she listened and soon took positive steps toward building a stronger relationship with her husband.

We may not experience such drastic problems in our marriages, but we may fall prey to the comparison trap. It may happen in church when we notice a husband put his arm lovingly around his wife and give her an affectionate squeeze—and we wish our husbands would be as affectionate as hers. Or we may observe another husband playing ball with his children and wish ours would spend more time playing with our children. A husband may notice his buddy's home is always clean and silently wish his wife would do a better job in his. It's all too easy to look at another marriage and find our own lacking.

We need to remember that we never have all the facts about another marriage. An affectionate husband may not help with the kids. The playful father may have difficulty communicating with his wife. The tidy wife may struggle in her relationship with her children. It may all look perfect from the outside, but there is no perfect relationship.

The danger of the comparison trap is that it can promote dissatisfaction. We are to learn from one another's marriages and to be encouraged by them, but at the same time, we must remember that every marriage is different.

The Hopeless Trap

We've all heard the axiom, "Don't go into marriage thinking you can change your mate. You can't."

This is good, solid advice for those considering marriage. On the other hand, after the wedding, hope can give way to desperation when a spouse realizes, "My mate will never change—our situation can't be helped." Such hopelessness can lead to defeated resignation that causes one marriage partner to quit trying.

Several years ago at a conference, a young couple asked John and me if we would meet with them. Apparently their marriage was in a real rut. With a large income, lovely children, and a common faith, it appeared they had everything going for them. But they were miserable. At least, she was miserable. Unhappy with his schedule and his lack of attention to her and the children, she appeared to be sliding steadily into marital hopelessness. After talking to the couple for some time, we asked the husband about his goals in life. He responded that he wanted to be the best stockbroker and the best tennis player in his age bracket in the state. An honest man, he acknowledged that cultivating family relationships was probably not as important to him as it should be.

John and I left them feeling that we had not been very helpful and that unless God worked a miracle, the marriage was doomed. Change didn't seem likely, but we prayed anyway. Four years went by and we didn't hear any more about them until two weeks ago when our doorbell rang. They were visiting our town and decided to drop by and tell us how happy they were because God had revived their marriage and family life. The wife said, "My husband is a changed man."

I have a friend who is married to a man whose ideas about God are quite different from her own. Besides that, they have different values about many things. With a house full of children, hers is a challenging situation. We get together quite often to encourage and pray for one another. For some time, we prayed for her husband's relationship with his son. He didn't seem to spend much time with the boy and they were not close. In all honesty, even though we prayed, we weren't too hopeful that he would change. But just recently she phoned to say, "I can't believe it, but my husband has been going to all of our son's ball games." This may seem like a little step, but a small step is a beginning. Hope is small steps taken one at a time.

Our God is God of the impossible. He is the One who can bring about change and growth in anyone. We need not remain in the hopeless trap. We must not give up on our mates or on ourselves.

From time to time, each of us will fall into the picky trap, the comparison trap, and even the hopeless trap. If we want to build a strong friendship with our mates, we must be aware of these traps, seek to avoid them, and focus instead on three gems that will encourage our marriage friendships.

Three Gems to Polish in a Marriage Friendship

A Thankful Spirit

It wasn't much fun to come face-to-face with my own picky nature. But God is full of mercy and as I began to confess my critical spirit, He began to remind me that my focus was wrong. Instead of focusing on the positive things about my husband, I was unconsciously choosing to dwell on the negatives. What I needed was a fresh infusion of a thankful spirit.

If each day we thank God for one or two specific things we appreciate about our mate, our hearts will begin to be filled with gratitude rather than criticism. In addition, tell your mate, each day, something that you appreciate. It's all too easy to take someone for granted rather than to appreciate him.

John has always been incredibly disciplined about getting up early to prepare for the day, to pray, and to read the Bible for guidance. He prays for specific things in each of our children's lives and in my life. I've always taken this for granted. It's just something he does. But recently I realized I should tell him how much it means to me. When I did, he was pleased and I was filled with a fresh sense of gratitude for this amazing man.

For years, I've been in a prayer group with my friend Holly. Our focus in this particular group is to pray for our children's schools. But invariably, each time we pray, Holly spends time praying for our husbands, thanking God that they work hard to support us and that they want to be good husbands and fathers and asking God to bless them. Her prayers have a wonderful way of reminding all of us to have a thankful spirit.

Titus 2:4 says that older women are to teach younger women to love their husbands. Holly's prayers do this; so does her counsel to younger women. A thankful heart doesn't mean, "Everything's fine because we just praise the Lord." Things may be rotten. Loving, honest confrontation may be needed. Counseling may be crucial. But day in and day out we are going to build a strong marriage friendship only if we choose to cultivate a thankful spirit.

An Accepting Atmosphere

Robert Frost in his poem "Death of the Hired Man" writes, "Home is where when you go there, they have to take you in." But home is even more than that. It should be the place that you can't wait to go to at the end of the day. Are our homes places that our families can't wait to get to each evening? As our spouse drives home, is he eager to see his family? Is he looking forward to getting there? Am I eagerly waiting for him? Or if I am the one who has been gone all day, do I eagerly look forward to an evening reunion with my mate?

The atmosphere in our homes will either encourage or discourage the building of strong marriage friendships. Our homes should, above all, be a place of acceptance—a place where we don't have to worry about measuring up. A place where we are loved simply because we belong.

A simple greeting at the end of the day can set the tone for the rest of the evening in our homes. Coming home can be a time of celebration. I've found it helpful for the mate who gets home first to stop whatever he is doing and rise to greet the arriving spouse with a celebration hug. It's often easier to keep reading the paper or fixing the supper, but an enthusiastic greeting at the front door is nonverbal communication that says, "I'm so glad you are here." That's acceptance.

An accepting atmosphere also allows for the freedom of honesty. It enables us to deal with conflict because we are committed to the covenant. We remember that we are on the same team and God is on our side.

An accepting atmosphere stresses service rather than roles. "It's the woman's job to . . . " or "It's the man's job to . . . " is not the basis for a relationship. Rather, we are *both* called to serve one another. *He* may need to cook dinner. *She* may need to pay the bills and do the taxes. The questions to ask are, *What can I do to make my partner's life easier? How can I better serve my partner?*

Often it's the little things that indicate our desire to please and serve our mates. A wife who takes the time to freshen up before her husband walks in is saying, *You are important. I want to look nice for you.*

A husband who makes time to clean the inside of his wife's dirty car is communicating that he cares for her. When we serve one another, we are honoring our mates, and such honor will cause our marriage friendships to deepen.

An accepting atmosphere is one in which mates express an interest in each other. When we spend the day apart and come together in the evening, exhausted by the demands of our day, it can be easy to relax and tune out. After all, we're home and we're accepted. Right? Yes, but that doesn't mean we can get so relaxed that we fail to express a genuine interest in our mates.

Simply asking good questions indicates that we care about our spouses. Too often our conversations go:

"How was your day?"

"Fine. How was yours?"

"Okay. What's for supper?"

Then after we get the kids to bed, we fall into bed exhausted, only to get up early to face another full day.

Many wives complain that their husbands don't talk to them—don't share with them on a deep level. I believe the reason is simply that often we don't ask good questions. "What was something that made you feel particularly happy or satisfied today?" is a sample of a good question that might lead to a deeper conversation.

Sometimes our mates don't discuss difficulties with us because we have too many answers. An exhausted mother of toddlers may tell her husband about her long day of nursing kids, cleaning, and disciplining, and in her frustration she may comment that she doesn't even like one of their children. She doesn't need him to respond with a plan for her day or an idea for improving her relationship with the difficult child! She needs empathy and appreciation. A husband struggling with a project doesn't necessarily want three easy solutions from his wife. He just needs a listening ear. As mates we must resist the tendency to fix everything in each other's lives and pray for wisdom to know when to advise and when to simply listen.

A Fresh Vision for Our Marriages

When we said, "I do," at the altar, we weren't saying, "I've arrived; now I can sit back and enjoy living life happily ever after." What we were really saying was, "I *do* promise to work at this relationship for the rest of my life." The marriage ceremony isn't like graduation; rather, it's similar to the first day of kindergarten! It's not the culmination, but the beginning.

Each marriage will go through different seasons, and each season will have distinct challenges and specific blessings. Newlyweds have the challenge of considering another person's desires when they are used to focusing only on their own. But they soon discover the joys of married life as they learn to care for each other.

The arrival of a first child ushers in a different season in marriage and brings with it the challenge of sacrificing the couple's wants to care for the needs of a baby. Both mates are challenged to learn flexibility, for life with a young child is unpredictable. Even though caring for an infant can be taxing, there is a wonderful blessing in watching this treasure that is yours together begin to respond to your love.

The season of having children at home brings many challenges. One is finding time to cultivate our marriage relationships. There *never* seems to be enough time. We are forced to reorder our priorities and determine what really matters in family life. That reordering brings blessings to our marriages.

Each season of marriage is different. Recognizing the challenges and blessings of the changing seasons gives us perspective on our marriages. No season lasts forever. Our circumstances change and we grow. Some seasons are more challenging than others. The benefit lies in working through the challenges and focusing on the blessings. Ask God to give you a fresh vision for the season you are in right now.

Fresh vision often comes when we recognize our gifts and begin to develop them. We want to be with those who bring out the best in us and encourage us. Our mates know us better than anyone else, and we know our mates better than anyone else. A blessing we can give each other is to discuss and to encourage one another's gifts.

Bill was in commercial development. He had a lot of experience and loved building projects. But when the economy turned downward, his work became discouraging. His wife, Robin, encouraged him to become involved in their church's new building program. Not being deeply absorbed in the church, he was a bit hesitant at first. But, with her support, he did. In fact, he became the head of the church's multimillion-dollar building program. Encouraged by his wife, Bill used his talents to help his church; in the process, his faith blossomed, his family relationships deepened, and his sense of personal fulfillment increased.

My friend Ann has a wonderful counseling gift. She has an uncanny ability to help women who are struggling to believe in God or struggling with relationships. Her husband has noticed this gift, and he encourages it by taking care of the boys so she can meet with different women.

Women who have chosen to stay home with their children face a new season in their lives when the last child leaves home. It's a wise husband who foresees the adjustments this will bring and encourages his wife to begin thinking about a new career *before* their children leave. They could have a date together and discuss her interests. Perhaps as the children get older he could encourage her to take some classes or begin working part-time. Often when a mom has put her own gifts and interests on hold for a number of years, she experiences a lack of confidence about reentering the workplace. Now, more than ever, she needs her husband's loving support and confidence-building words.

A fresh vision for a marriage relationship includes having creative fun. As we encourage and support one another in the development of our gifts, we simply must remember to take time for fun. Life is filled with serious issues, and it can easily become an exhausting existence. "Too tired to have fun" might be an accurate statement of marriages today. What a shame! Perhaps some of these simple, fun ideas might help:

- Plan a weekly date alone, together. An evening out or a breakfast date will allow time to cultivate your marriage friendship.
- Curl up together on the couch one night a week after the kids are in bed. Light candles, eat a special dessert, and discuss more than the calendar and the children.
- Develop common hobbies. A friend recently took up tennis because her husband likes to play. She took lessons and now the two of them play together.
- Take turns planning an adventure of the month. It may be a play, an all-day hike and a picnic, or some other creative activity. It's more fun if the planning partner keeps the activity a surprise until the day of the event.
- Curl up on a couch and spend an evening looking at old photos together.
- Usher at a concert together. You usually get in for free.
- Plan a "King/Queen for the Day" event. Enlist the children's help in honoring your spouse by serving him or her breakfast in bed, writing love notes, and doing your mate's chores. Add your own and your kids' ideas for honoring your mate.
- Take a blanket outside, curl up together, and watch the stars come out.

- Bake cookies or hot pretzels together. Send some in a surprise package to a friend simply to say, "We appreciate your friendship."
- Put on your favorite old music, move the furniture, and dance together. Invite the kids to join in. It's guaranteed to produce laughter.
- Buy a book of love poems and read them aloud to each other.
- Surprise your mate by kidnapping him or her from work. Coordinate this with a secretary or coworkers. Arrange your baby-sitting ahead of time, go out to dinner, and stay away overnight.

A thankful spirit, an accepting atmosphere, and a fresh vision will encourage us as we continue to cultivate friendships with our mates. We must remember, however, that while we're on this earth, we will never get to the place of a perfect relationship with our partner. Author Larry Crabb says that there is no perfect relationship this side of heaven. He contends that even in the most ideal marriage there will still be a little restlessness. This is how God intended it, because our deepest longing for a totally fulfilling relationship will be met only when we are with Him in heaven.

Too many people go from mate to mate looking for what they cannot find. Instead, we must rejoice in the mate God has given us, remembering that He has given us the partner we need to help us become the person He intended for us to be.

That day, curled up by the smoldering ashes of the fire, I knew I needed to call my husband. I didn't especially want to, but I knew it was the right thing to do. When I got him on the phone, I said, "Honey, I need to apologize to you. I don't feel like I've been a very good friend to you lately. Will you forgive me?" Of course he did, but more importantly, I had a change of heart.

Marriage friendships will not grow unless we practice asking for and granting forgiveness. Forgiveness is the cornerstone of our faith and the hope for revitalized relationships.

Focus Questions

Meditate on 1 Corinthians 13.

1. List the different characteristics of love. Ask God to show you where *you* are weak in your relationship with your mate. Begin to pray that He will help you in these areas. Be encouraged by 2 Corinthians 12:9.

2. Pray for your mate and the concerns that you know he or she has. Praise God for the qualities in your mate that you admire. Write a note to your mate sharing specific things that you are thankful for in him or her.

Family Friendship Builder

Plan a surprise date for your mate and yourself during the next two weeks. Do something you know your *mate* would like.

Friendships Between Parents and Young Children

He tends his flock like a shepherd:
He gathers the lambs in his arms
And carries them close to his heart;
He gently leads those that have young.

Isaiah 40:11

T his week my husband is out of town. I've been on
the phone, long distance, with an old friend who was
in tears over a broken relationship. While trying to
counsel her, my one-year-old twins climbed on the kitchen
counter, emptied a bottle of Elmer's glue, sticking it all over
themselves, the phone books, notes, and everything in sight.
The blond fuzz on their little heads became stiff spikes. Just
as I was getting the girls into the tub, Chris poured John's
box of Cracker Jacks down the carpeted steps. Then John
started yelling at Chris to clean them up, and Chris stubbed
his toe and began crying. All I want to do is run away!

I wrote this in my journal during those exhausting days when the children were young. In our household, chaos hit either when I was on the phone or during *arsenic hours*—the three hours between 4 P.M. and 7 P.M. Arsenic hours is that terrible time of the day when you're tired, the kids are tired, and it's turning into a very long day.

I have a clear picture in my mind of one day right before this poisonous time. I was very tired and I was dreading the next couple of hours. I desperately wanted to be a good mother, but I just wasn't sure I had it in me at the moment. As I sat on the couch trying to summon up fresh strength, eight-year-old Allison came and stood beside me.

"Allison," I said, "I'm so tired. I'm afraid I might be a very bad mother in the next couple of hours. Would you pray for me?"

"Dear Jesus," she prayed, putting her arms around me, "please help Mommy and help her have patience." Oh, she encouraged my heart! I needed my young child's prayers.

The years when you parent young children can be the most challenging of all the parenting years. You work so hard, yet you see so few results. Children don't become obedient overnight, siblings don't always like each other, and parents often feel unappreciated. But these early years are the most crucial in laying the foundation for the friendships we want to build within our families.

Eight Foundation Builders

Several years ago, we began construction on a new church building. In the beginning, the workmen dug a big pit in the ground and then they began to pour footings. Footings are cement piers upon which the entire building rests. They are crucial to the strength of the finished structure. After the foundation hole is dug, the footings must be poured quickly, before the composition of the soil is changed by the wind, air, or water.

In a similar way in these brief early years, parents of young children have the challenging job of laying the foundation that will support family friendships in later years. Here are eight "foundation builders" to help parents as they seek to cultivate strong friendships with their young children.

1. Hug Them and Praise Them
Physical affection and verbal affirmation are necessary in laying a strong foundation for friendship. Hug, hug, hug. Even if you were not

raised in a hugging family, hug your kids anyway. They need the warmth of physical contact and so do you. From gently rocking the tiny infant to hugging a preadolescent, physical touch communicates love and provides security. Encourage your kids to hug each other as well. Let them begin by holding a newborn brother or sister.

Say "I love you" and say it often. When we talk with our children, it's meaningful if we look them in the eyes. So squat down to their level when you truly want to communicate with them, and let them know that what you are saying to one another is important. Praise them for little things. "That was so nice when you complimented your brother for the pretty picture he drew." Praise them for big things. "You did such a good job helping me clean up."

But we must be genuine in our praise. Tony Campolo warns that with our society's intense focus on building self-esteem, we must take care not to praise mediocrity. We can overdo affirmation, and if it is undeserved, it sends a wrong message to the child. And that's not true integrity. Seek to be balanced in your praise of your children. Praise your children often and train them in excellence.

2. See Discipline as an Asset

My nephew Frank is four years old. His favorite line these days is, "If you don't let me . . . I won't be your friend anymore."

The threat is his ultimate weapon to get his own way. Just his choice of words makes you feel as if you are working at cross-purposes with him. I want to be friends with this child, but he must learn he can't always have or do what he wants. He must also learn that I love him even when I don't give him what he wants. It's the age-old dilemma: Are discipline and love compatible?

Yes, they are; in fact, one is necessary for the other. Discipline is not the enemy of love and friendship; rather, it is a key to healthy relationships. As we discussed in an earlier chapter, discipline leads to respect, and respect encourages friendship.

A young child will try to manipulate and be in charge. He will attempt to get his own way. While the child may not be consciously trying to control, this is what he is doing. A wise parent must not permit this to happen. Letting a child manipulate or control puts an awful, unfair burden on the child. Firm discipline relieves a child of this burden and builds respect for the parent. When a child respects his parents, he will also respect others.

Firm discipline and love aren't opposites, but today many well-meaning parents are unintentionally acting as if they are. Some of these parents have come from abusive homes in which the discipline was overwhelming or even cruel. To them *any* kind of discipline is abusive. In an effort to not repeat the mistakes of their parents, they have thrown out discipline and instead attempt to placate the child. There is no way you can reason with a strong-willed two-year-old. Your toddler must learn that "no" means "no" and not "maybe, if you fuss enough."

If you want to build a friendship with your child, firm discipline is essential, especially in the early years. Many teenage difficulties can be avoided by exercising firm discipline when the child is young. If discipline and love were confused in *your* childhood home, it may be helpful to get some advice from a trained counselor so that you will not repeat the mistakes your parents made.

Even if you seek help, you will *still* make mistakes, because we all make mistakes in training our children. We must have a humble spirit that allows us to confess to our children, "I was wrong. I am so sorry. Will you forgive me?" On the flip side, though, we must remember that we are not running for "the most popular parent in town." Our job is not to make sure that our kids are always happy; rather, it is to raise them to become responsible adults who care for one another. Keep this long-range goal in view.

3. Create Traditions

Tradition and discipline are related, for tradition begins with a regularly scheduled event and the repetition, time after time, of that event. Discipline, too, is the repetition of many small acts until they become ingrained as part of the way in which a child relates to the world. Small children need a schedule—a routine. Schedules build confidence in children because they know what to expect and when to expect it.

A daily schedule with toddlers might be: breakfast with the parents, playtime alone, snack or lunch, nap, afternoon outing, playtime with a parent, dinner, storytelling, bedtime.

Schedules differ in each household, but the emphasis should always be on trying to have a daily routine. Sometimes this might not be possible, but as much as you can, set up a routine. Scheduling will make your life easier and will teach your children the benefits of discipline.

Little traditions or disciplines might include a daily craft time with

Mommy at the kitchen table, snuggling in Dad's cuddling chair for that special time to read each evening, or playing a game for a few minutes at the same time each day.

When my brother-in-law comes home from work, he has the tradition of playing chase around the family room couch with his young kids. They must each touch the couch, but then they can run in any direction to avoid Dad. This game lasts about five minutes, but the hysterical laughter and fun is a building block to friendships that will last a lifetime.

Each night when my friend Lolly puts her young son to bed, she has a game in which she traces alphabet messages with her finger on his back, and he tries to guess what she is writing.

In another family, the young children take turns making up bedtime stories for the parents each night.

Besides daily traditions, special traditions also build memories. We discovered a special tradition by accident. When Allison was eight, she and I took a train to New York City. Both of us needed a break from the four younger kids. We had 24 hours together, completely alone. We played games on the train, went sight-seeing in the city, and saw the newly released musical *Annie*.

I knew it had been a special time when we returned home and that night I found her crying at bedtime. "What's the matter, honey?" I asked with concern.

"Mommy, I was just thinking about how wonderful our trip was," she responded.

That memory was so special to each of us that John and I decided to make it a tradition. When the children were close to eight years of age, I took each of them away alone for an overnight trip. And when they neared 13, John did the same thing. Each trip was different and each became a special memory.

Our friend Larry travels for his business, but everywhere he goes he sends home postcards to his two young sons. Mail time is very special and their postcard collections are growing. Most important, they know their dad is thinking of them no matter where he goes.

When we play with young children, we set the stage for talking with them when they are older. It's easier to do this with the first child, because by the time the third or fourth comes along, we are tired of that same old book or that same old game. This is just natural parental burnout. So

those of us with large families have to ask God for extra energy to
continue these important traditions. The youngest child in the family needs
interaction as much as the oldest did.

On the other hand, the parent of an only child has unique challenges.
While that child needs special traditions with his parents, he must also
learn to entertain himself. Having friends over can provide some relief, as
well as teach the only child valuable lessons about sharing, taking turns,
and doing what another child wants first.

4. Cultivate Laughter

One of the things I most want my children to remember is laughing
together. Playing "Sardines" in the dark has always caused laughter at our
house. We turn out all the lights in the house and one person hides. Other
family members are the finders, and as each finds the hidden person, he or
she quietly hides too, until everyone has discovered the hidden person or
group! It's hysterical to play together, especially when several people are
hiding in a tiny place and no one can see anything!

As we learn to laugh at ourselves, we will help our children learn to laugh
at themselves. Once I made a birthday cake from scratch for John. The flour
had bugs in it and I used the wrong kind of oil. It was lopsided, sprinkled
with bugs, and gross tasting. But he made the whole situation so funny that
we all laughed and dubbed it "Mom's famous recipe—made once."

When my friend Heidi was in third grade, a school bully began to sing
"Heidi, Heidi Hippo!" parroting a popular song of the time. Every day for
many days she came home from school in tears. Her mom hugged her and
said, "You have to learn to laugh with them and at yourself."

Then her mom bought some bright green fabric and made a stylish
skirt with a hippo on it. Heidi wore it to school, and for a day she laughed
with her friends. That was the end of the teasing. Today at 23 she remembers this as a great lesson: If you can laugh at yourself and with other
people, you will save yourself a lot of heartache, and you will learn not to
take yourself too seriously. It's no surprise that one of her gifts is a great
sense of humor.

A boy was having a discussion with his mom about some of his relationships at school. He commented to her, "My friend is so funny. He makes
everyone laugh and all the kids like him. I wish I were funny like that."

"Son," she responded, "we can't all be funny. Funny people need
people like you to laugh at their humor. Your laughter is a gift to them."

Our humor should be positive and not filled with sarcasm. It's too easy to fall into a cynical, sarcastic type of humor that is destructive. Laugh at yourself and pray for a sense of humor in your home.

5. Stay Close to Teachers

Many elementary schools have parent-teacher conferences near the beginning of the year. This is a wonderful opportunity to get to know the teacher who will be influencing your child for the next school term.

Seek to build positive relationships with your child's teachers. Ask how you can be supportive of them. And let them know that you want them to call with any concerns they have about your child. Tell them you are interested not only in your child's academic development, but in his character development as well.

We once had a teacher phone us because she felt our twins were being unusually cliquey with certain friends while leaving others out. I appreciated her call, and we began to work together with the girls to overcome this tendency. It was a valuable learning experience for all.

Go on field trips with your child's class. One dad in our community tries to go on most of the field trips in which his kids participate. It enables him to be in their world, observing them with their friends, and it gives him a common interest with his kids.

6. Be Where They Are

The license plate said, "My Home." And that's the way many of us feel during the carpooling years—as if we live in the car. But that's not all bad. The car is a great place to listen to your children talk with their friends. You can hear things you would never hear when talking to them alone. The car pool can be a research lab if you take time to listen and ask good questions. You can learn who did the "baddest" thing and who spit at whom. You can discover who likes whom and what teacher is the "meanest." You can pick up on attitudes and trends, information that they are accumulating that is "right on," and misinformation that needs to be corrected.

When we take our children and other kids to a park and watch them interact, we get to know our own children and their friends in even more ways. Do our children initiate games or feel more comfortable following others? Do they like constant activity or quiet playtime? Are they risk takers or fearful when trying new things? Do they laugh easily or are they more serious?

Parents need to build friendships with their children's friends. In this way they come to truly understand their own children. It's not hard to build those friendships. Tell your daughter's friend you like her haircut. Ask your son's friend what his favorite sport is. Cheer for your children's friends and tell your children what you appreciate about their friends. (I appreciate the twins' friend Christina, who always smiles and gives me a hug.)

If you appreciate and work at getting to know your children's friends when they are young, the teenage years will be much easier. You will already know most of them and your children will be accustomed to having you relate with their friends.

7. Share Your Life with Them

When I asked Allison at age eight to pray for me, I genuinely needed her help. She knew from experience that the next couple of hours were going to be wild, and Mommy really *did* need patience.

Children know that their parents are not always right. No one is. What they need is parents who are willing to be truthful and admit their mistakes. They need parents who recognize their own need for God.

Perhaps you grew up in a home where there was no spiritual training. As a result, it seems awkward to pray with your young children. Children can ask questions about spiritual matters that even Solomon might have had trouble answering. When you feel inadequate in answering their questions or uncomfortable praying with them, simply be honest. Tell them that there is a lot you don't know yet. The two of you will have to try to find the answers together.

Take time to share the things you ponder in your own heart with your child. In our busy lives, it's all too easy to communicate just the functional—who has to be where and when, and what homework has to be done. The child needs to know what's going on in your heart and mind, too. "You know, I've been thinking a lot about . . . " When we share our hearts with young children, it will open the door for them to communicate at a deeper level with us as they mature.

Another way to deepen communication with your children is to practice asking deeper questions.

"Can you tell me one thing that made you feel happy today?"

"Joannie, if you had a friend who wanted to copy answers from your paper, what would you do?"

"Why do you suppose God wanted people to 'remember the Sabbath'?"

8. Keep a Long-Range Perspective

The construction left a big, muddy hole on our church grounds. It was ugly, it was yucky, and it was hard to imagine a beautiful new church building full of people singing glorious hymns on the site. Progress crawled. It rained and rained and no work could be done. Building materials were delayed, and when they did arrive, they were often the wrong materials or cut to the wrong dimensions. Finally, the project was progressing. Then, by mistake, someone drove a stake through a major pipe. Water poured out everywhere and the floor had to be redone. Discouragement came easily. The workers had to laugh, press on, and keep the final picture in mind.

Parents of young children sometimes feel much like those workers. We work and work and don't see much progress. Or we make progress in one area and then have a setback in another. It's easy to lose our perspective and become discouraged. We have to remember that we are laying the foundation for a child's future life and friendships and it can be a tedious process. Our children are tender shoots full of the promise of great things. As we gently train and steer them, we need a long-range perspective.

In a way, these early years are similar to taking out a savings bond. We put much into our children's lives, but we don't see much return on our initial investment for several years. In the same way we expect our monetary investments to pay off in the future, we have to remember we are building for our children's futures.

When we feel discouraged, we need to remember that our heavenly Father loves our children even more than we do and He knows our shortcomings. He will gently train *us* as we train them, and we will all grow in mutual dependence upon Him.

Focus Questions

Meditate on Psalms 130 and 131.

1. As parents of young children, we often feel like failures. What do you read here that encourages you?
2. The words *hope* and *wait* are used frequently in Psalm 130. What do those words mean to you?
3. Psalm 131:2 reminds us that we are to be like children in our relationships with God. As you observe your children, what do you learn from them about your relationship with God?

Family Friendship Builder

Write a letter to your child sharing the ways in which God is using him to teach you. Thank the child for the truths he has brought to your mind as you have raised him. Save this letter and give it to your child when he is older.

CHAPTER 10

Friendships Between Siblings

Show me your ways, O Lord,
teach me your paths;
Guide me in your truth and teach me,
for you are God my Savior,
and my hope is in you all day long.

Psalm 25:4, 5

Roars poured from the family room, where Will and Tad were arguing. Their dad realized that this noise wasn't the typical give-and-take of boys at play. Going to check out what was happening, he paused to watch quietly from the door. The boys' emotions were at fever pitch and a genuine fist fight appeared to be imminent.

"You ——!" Tad, the younger son, yelled at his brother in complete frustration. The curse words he used were not allowed in this household. Breaking up the argument, Dad took Tad aside and said, "Son, you know those words are unacceptable. You will have to go to your room."

"But Will made me say it," wailed the furious child, "and you're punishing me, not Will, and it's all his fault. Why aren't you punishing him?"

"*Nobody* makes you talk like that. *You* are responsible for what comes out of *your* mouth, son. Your brother is not," replied Dad.

"I hate my brother."

Sound familiar? Scenes such as this happen every day in homes everywhere, and exhausted parents are asking themselves, "Did I handle this right? Will these children ever like each other? Why do they always think I'm unfair? Will they ever appreciate me, their battered parent?"

The issue of sibling rivalry has been around forever. The Old Testament tells a story about sibling rivalry. Because Joseph's brothers were jealous, they threw him into a pit to die. Years later, after he had been miraculously rescued from the pit, taken to Egypt, and given a position of leadership directly under Pharaoh, Joseph saved his brothers and their families from a severe famine. About this rather drastic conflict between brothers, the Bible says, "What [the brothers] meant for evil, God used for good" (Gen. 50:20).

While the causes of sibling rivalry are many, they can be reduced to one basic source—original sin. We all want *what* we want *when* we want it. *We* want to be the favorite. *We* want everything to go our way. *We* want the most recognition. *We* want the most attention. And we *don't want* to share, wait, or let someone else get the credit!

Every family experiences the frustration of sibling rivalry to some degree. It's natural. Since no two families are exactly alike, the degree of sibling rivalry will vary and will be influenced by the sexes of the children, their age differences, their personalities, their birth order, and how the parents handle problems.

The purpose of this chapter is not to analyze all the causes of jealousy and disputes between brothers and sisters, but instead, to look at positive ways of encouraging friendship in the midst of normal rivalries and arguments. Our job as parents is not merely to keep our kids from disliking each other, but to give them the tools for learning how to be friends. Sometimes, all we can do is keep young rivals apart and keep them from killing each other. Even though we may be weary of the struggle to build family friendships, we must keep encouraging our children toward positive attitudes and actions that will help them grow to love one another and to be friends.

Our greatest desire must be that our kids will love the Lord with all their hearts, love us as their parents, and love each other as well. It's so important that our children become friends with each other. They will not always have us, their parents, to turn to in times of crisis and need. Some day the older generation will pass away, but if siblings have become friends, they will have each other. Nothing brings a parent greater joy than watching two brothers who once fought about almost everything now give each other a bear hug and take off to spend an afternoon together.

Because the challenges of dealing with sibling rivalry are different at every age, let's look at some ways of building friendships between brothers and sisters at three important stages of their lives: the early, middle, and later (teen) years.

The Early Years

They had brought the new baby home from the hospital just a few days earlier. Friends and relatives had been by to see him, and the pile of baby presents on the dining room table had grown steadily. After an exhausting morning, Mom once again picked up the fussy infant and rocked him, trying to quiet him. The baby's toddler sister dragged her blanket over to her mother's chair. "Take baby back now, Mommy," she said with an exasperated voice. "He go bye-bye now."

To this toddler, the new baby had intruded long enough! Her schedule had been upset, her parents were distracted and exhausted, and she was no longer the center of attention. Hers was the typical reaction of an older sibling.

A newborn will be the focus of attention in any home. This is especially true for a first child. The exhausted parents struggle to make the many adjustments and grow in confidence in caring for a baby. I have always thought that the first child is the hardest, because parents don't know what they're doing, and they either get too much advice or not enough.

No child should remain the center of attention in the family for very long. Children must learn early in life that they are *not* the center of the universe. This is the first step in leading them away from a self-centered life toward one that is intent on serving others.

The early childhood years are important. During this time, the seeds of character are beginning to develop. Personality qualities such as patience, thoughtfulness, gentleness, and caring begin to develop at this age.

Here are practical tips for relieving some of the natural rivalry between siblings and helping them to develop an appreciation for one another.

Prepare for the Homecoming of a New Sibling

When a new baby is due soon, begin preparing an older child for the baby's arrival. Bolster your older child's self-esteem often. Give him or her a positive vision for what a good older sibling he or she will be. Say, "You are going to be the best big brother this little baby could ever have. I am so proud of you." Or, "This new baby is so lucky to have you for a sister. You are going to be able to teach him so many things."

Don't be shocked when the new baby is a disappointment to an older child. After all, that little baby isn't much fun to play with. Remind the older child that the baby will grow up soon, and then they can run all over and play together.

Make Bringing the New Baby Home Special

When John and I brought each of our five children home, we laid the new baby on the couch and had family members put their hands on the infant as we prayed. In prayer we gave back to the Lord this very special child He had given us. We asked God to keep him safe and we asked that he would grow to love the Lord. Then we asked the Lord to help us to learn how to be good parents, brothers, or sisters for the new member of our family.

When worries about the baby would arise, this family dedication time was important to me. I held in my mind the picture of our family giving this child back to the Lord. It helped me remember whose child he was.

Have the Baby Bring a Gift to the Siblings at Home

Before I went to the hospital to have a baby, I bought gifts for each older child and wrapped them. These were gifts from the new baby to the brothers and sisters at home. The gifts stayed in the car trunk until the day the baby and I came home. Then I handed each sibling a note of love and a gift from the new brother or sister.

Have an Activity Box for the Older Children

Older siblings often misbehave when Mom or Dad is taking care of the new baby. A special activity box can help at those times. Fill a plastic box with markers, stickers, paper, and other tools for creativity, and keep it in a specific place. This is the "big boy" or "big girl" box, and it comes out only when Mommy is busy with the new baby. A big brother or sister is the only one who can have this special box.

Allison was two when John was born, and she got a new doll from her brother. When I nursed John, she would often get her "baby" out and "nurse" it. We talked about what a great mother she was going to be one day and what a good big sister she was now to be so patient while Mommy took care of John. At least *her* baby didn't fuss!

Take the Older Children on Outings All by Themselves

Older children resent the time a baby takes, but special outings with Mom or Dad can lessen the feelings. Leave the baby with a sitter and take the older child out for ice cream. Take him to a playground or a fast food restaurant. Let him stay up to watch an appropriate video with you. This doesn't completely solve the problem, but when those times of resentment come and the older child expresses his negative feelings, remind him of your special dates with him alone.

Set Clear Standards of Behavior During the Early Years

Just as the young child wanted her mommy to take the new baby back, we all want others to make changes so that our life-styles are a little more comfortable—so that our own desires will be satisfied. We are basically self-centered, and we will never completely get over it this side of heaven. When the standards of acceptable behavior are clear to our young children, they will know how we expect them to relate to one another. Be clear, firm, and consistent with discipline.

Teach Young Children to Wait

Teaching a child to wait for attention is no fun. It's tough on the parents and it's tough on the child. He won't like it. He may fuss or throw a temper tantrum, but he must learn to wait. God will use a new baby as an instrument to help us teach our younger children they must wait for Mommy's attention.

We all want immediate satisfaction of our needs. Learning at a young age to wait is a good thing. So when you hear wails of protest from your child—that he dislikes the new baby because you can't take care of his needs first—take heart. Your child is only learning that the world doesn't revolve around him. That's a good thing!

Teach Young Children to Take Turns and Share

It always happens. There's a toy no one has wanted to play with and then someone finds it and everyone wants it at the same time. The typical struggle ensues. As far as I'm concerned, a timer with a bell is essential in homes with young children. Give each child a set time to play with the toy over which they are fighting. One child can have it until the bell rings, and then it's another child's turn.

The debate over who gets to sit next to the window on a three-minute car ride can begin a sibling war. Who would ever imagine something so trivial can be so disruptive? Yet, in nearly every family, such debate can cause real trouble.

A friend of mine solved this dilemma by assigning one child all the odd-numbered days. Her other child got the even days. On a child's assigned day, he got first choice at everything all day long. This simple system has changed their family life! (If you have more than two children, assign one child every third or fourth day. On that day he gets first choice of everything.)

Teach Children to Respect Other People's Property

Since I have already covered this thoroughly in an earlier chapter, I won't go into detail here. But if we fail to emphasize respecting others, we omit one of the most crucial building blocks in channeling sibling rivalry into sibling friendship.

Simply put: do not permit disrespect—not of parents, of those in authority, or of siblings. Family is the place where we stick up for one another. We will not always agree, but we must learn to disagree politely.

Teach your children to respect and care for each other's toys. The one who took the soccer ball out and forgot to bring it in should go get it— even if it is dark, even if he doesn't want to. Toddlers are too young to understand the difference between their property and that of big brothers and sisters. To avoid conflict, put big kids' toys out of the reach of destructive toddlers.

Teach Children to Look Out for Each Other

When a younger child falls on the playground, train the older ones to run to him, pick him up, and give him a hug. As they get older, expect them to stand up for each other.

Eugenia is two years younger than her brother. When they were in elementary school, another boy began to call Eugenia names and pull at her clothes. Eugenia told her big brother and he took the troublemaker aside and said, "That's my sister you are bothering. Don't you ever, ever bug her again."

Our message to our kids must be, "Brothers and sisters are our greatest treasures. Take care of them. Stand up for them."

This idea is most easily communicated when your children are young.

In the middle years, they may view each other more like a chronic embarrassment, or an impossible burden, than a great treasure.

The Middle Years

When Allison was 12 and her brother John was 10, they did not like each other very much. One day her class was doing science experiments at school. She brought home the eye of a cow that had been used in an experiment and told John it was a piece of candy. When he started to eat it, she burst out laughing and told him what it was. Needless to say, he was furious. But today at ages 19 and 21, they are best of friends. They both attend the University of Virginia, double-date, and take some classes together. How did they become friends? What happened? They grew up! But during those middle years we often wondered if they ever would be friends.

The standards of behavior that are set in the early years must be consistently enforced in the middle years. And that's exhausting! We second-guess how we are dealing with sibling rivalry. Are we handling it right? What about the fights? When is it right to get involved and when should we let them have it out?

Determine When to Get Involved and When Not to

A friend of mine, the mother of four boys, walked into the room where they were wrestling. She knew that before long one or two of them would come crying to her. "Okay, guys," she said, "if you insist on wrestling, I don't want to hear any complaints unless you can see blood or bones!"

We have to do the most intervention during the early years when we're setting standards of behavior. Young children need an involved coach when they first start to play a sport. They have to learn the rules in order to play properly and fairly and eventually to excel in their chosen sport. In a similar manner, young children must learn rules about the right way to treat others.

As children grow older, a parent can move from being involved as a coach to being a referee. Now the parent stands back and intervenes only when there is a clear violation of the rules. Later on, we will move away from an active place on the playing field and become spectators—watching our children interact, cheering their good moves, aching when they falter, but letting *them* make their own mistakes. Our job at that time is to ask good questions: "Can you think of three creative ways to handle this problem?" "If you were the parent, how would you handle this dispute?"

Sibling rivalry can be cruelest during the middle years, especially if no clear expectations about behavior and no consistent consequences have been applied during the earlier years. Parents are going to make mistakes and so are kids. Failure is a part of every family's life, and failure doesn't always have to be bad. Just remember that there are no mistakes that cannot be redeemed.

Anticipate Potential Conflicts

"She always gets to have a friend over and I never do."

"They won't let me play with them. They leave me out."

Until we've had some disastrous experiences, we probably won't learn what works or doesn't work in allowing our children to have friends over to play. When letting your children's friends come to your home turns out badly, it can be a learning experience about how to anticipate potential conflict and how to take steps to avoid it in the future.

After a negative experience, ask yourself some questions. What works best for our kids? Should each child have a friend over on the same day? Do they need to play in separate areas or do they play well together? Perhaps they can play separately and then together. Or would it be better for my children to take turns having a friend over?

You can use some of the time with the child who has no friend over to do something special, like playing a game. Or use the time for letting the child learn how to entertain himself. It is not the parents' job to entertain their children. They must learn to create their own entertainment.

Have Family Forums

Sometimes families experience repeated discord. When discord is the norm, it's time for a family forum. Gather the family together and insist that each person listen to every other family member express his views about the problem. Then discuss some creative solutions. Keep in mind that the goal is to attack the problem and not other family members. Before the family forum, parents need to agree about how they are going to handle the forum and what their goals are for it.

Be Sensitive to Physical and Emotional Changes

During these middle years, physical and emotional changes begin to take place. We'll look at this in greater detail in the next chapter, but it's important to anticipate this new season and to prepare our children for it. It can be a time of great embarrassment, and our children must learn that we will allow no teasing about the physical changes going on in a sibling's body. It's humiliating for a brother to have his sister make fun of his squeaky voice. When a younger sister develops before her older sister, the older one may wonder, *What's wrong with me?* It's helpful to remind our children that the "body is a temple of the Holy Spirit" (1 Cor. 6:19) and that it is "fearfully and wonderfully made" (Ps. 139:14). When and how they change is on God's timetable. This is the time for brothers and sisters to compliment and build one another up, not laugh at awkward changes.

Insist That Your Children Forgive and Accept Forgiveness
We were on a hike and Libby, who was carrying a big backpack, tripped and fell. She wasn't really hurt, but her older brother John began to laugh at her. What was really hurt were her feelings. As we continued our walk, the tension between the two increased until the whole family could feel it.

"John," we said, "you must tell Libby you are sorry and ask her to forgive you for making fun of her. It seems like a little thing, but your relationship is not right and we can't go any farther until you and Libby take care of this problem."

He didn't like doing it, but he did ask Libby for forgiveness. Both children learned an important lesson about forgiveness that day. People in families hurt each other and have to ask forgiveness. It may take time for feelings to heal, but forgiveness is the first step toward healing. We ask forgiveness, not because we feel like it, but because it's the right thing to do. (Teaching our children this principle will help them prepare for their own marriages, where the giving of, and asking for, forgiveness will be vitally important.) If there is no willingness to request and/or grant forgiveness, it may be necessary to withdraw privileges until there is.

Appreciate Unique Personalities
One of the twins came in the other day and said with exasperation, "Why does my sister like to talk on the phone all the time? I don't like to. She's weird."

"She's not weird," I responded. "You two are just different and I am so glad. It would be awful if you were just alike."

Frequently, our kids make comparisons of better or worse. The person or thing compared is not better or worse, but merely different. My mom often says of her 15 grandchildren, "It's so much fun and so interesting to see how different each child is."

Remind your children that they will have different skills and be good at different things. You help your child accept the level of his own and others' skills when you accept the child just as he is. Don't compare his grades with his siblings. Don't compare physical prowess or any other attribute of one child with another. Discussions about such matters need to be held in private with the child.

Be an Interpreter for Your Children

Your children might need someone to interpret what's troubling a sibling. Perhaps an adolescent girl is very moody and about to have her period. She is unusually cross with her younger brother. It's helpful to take the brother aside and simply explain that he's not the problem, female hormones are, and now's the time to stay out of her way and try to be extra nice. Her mood will pass.

However, if the behavior of one child becomes persistently negative and begins to damage the friendships within the family, parents *must* take action. Seek counsel from teachers, counselors, or your minister. If it's needed, get help! One child's behavior shouldn't negatively impact the entire family.

Provide Opportunities for Siblings to Work Together on Something Fun

Pairing up two of our children to plan a family scavenger hunt gave them an opportunity to work together on something positive. They had a lot of fun, and so did the rest of us as we tried to follow their clues and got stumped!

When two children who clash are put together on a project, they are given an opportunity to relate in a situation where they are not competing for Mom's, Dad's, or some other person's attention. An hour at the mall for two sisters may be a small step in forging a more positive relationship between them.

One idea is to put your children on the same sports team. Kelly, at seven, is a pistol. She likes to argue, is outgoing, and is fiercely competitive. Her nine-year-old brother Chad is quieter. He is equally competitive and has a temper. Kelly has a way of igniting his fuse. Their rivalry has exhausted their parents. But recently they played on the same soccer team. Finding a common interest has taught them to pull together instead of against one another and has had a positive impact on their entire relationship.

Prayerfully Consider the "Why" of Behavior

Many times I haven't known what to do nor have I been able to find answers about my child's behavior. Nothing that I tried worked, and I felt like an utter failure. I needed reassurance that God knew what was going on, and He would give me wisdom and redeem my mistakes. I have often prayed, "Lord, please give me some clues as to why these two don't get along. Please show me what to do."

Once again, the answer may often be found by asking questions. Is our family schedule too busy? Is a child overcommitted? Is he eating too much sugar or junk food? Is he getting enough sleep? Does the child need exercise? Do I need time alone with the child? Is there someone I could talk to whose child has already been through this stage and could give me some insights?

We may not get answers right away, but God will minister to us as we pray and are reminded, once again, that these are *His* kids first. He loves them more than we do, and He wants them to love each other.

The Later Years

Heidi and Rob are five years apart. During their early and middle years, the competition and bickering between them seemed endless. A simple Monopoly game could and often did turn into a screaming match as each tried to manipulate the rules. Because of their age difference, common interests were few and they didn't care a whole lot about spending time together. Even though it didn't seem the two were making much progress, their parents continued to work on the essentials necessary for a future friendship. They insisted the two attend each other's events; the whole family ate dinner together in the evening; and they did family activities together that provided all of them with pleasant memories for the later years.

One year Heidi was on the staff of a church camp in which Rob was a participant. During the camp they worked on a skit together and they realized that each of them was funny. A new appreciation for the other's talents developed.

Throughout the week, Heidi sought out Rob to ask him how he felt things were going at the camp. He might say to her, "You did a great job leading that discussion, Sis." That was the beginning of a new friendship between the two, and when she went off to college, they became even better friends.

One of the greatest blessings of our later years is watching seemingly impossible friendships start to blossom between members of our families. During these later childhood years, parents still play an important role in encouraging friendships between siblings.

Remind Your Children That They'll Get to Move Up Someday

When one child leaves home, it's time for new positions to be taken. The next child in line is suddenly the king or queen. This child may really begin to blossom as he or she moves to the head of the line and becomes the oldest child at home. Of course, when the college year ends or there is a furlough in military service and the missing oldest child is reinserted into family life, interesting challenges come up that are best met with lots of humor and grace.

Know What's Happening in Other Family Members' Lives

Pray together. Every morning at our house we take a few minutes for each person to share what's on his schedule for the day. We pray for one another. Then, in the evening during dinner, we often get a report of how everyone else's day went.

One of our biggest budget items is the phone bill. I don't worry about the cost, though, because it is an investment in family friendships. We pay for our calls to our kids, their calls home, and their calls to each other. (They are on their own for calls to friends.) Chris, who is a high school senior, often calls his brother, John, at college late at night. He asks about who he should ask out and what the subject of his English paper should be. It thrills me to hear the guys conferring with each other.

Clue Others In

Sometimes it's necessary to clue in one family member as to what's happening in another's life. When Chris was inducted into the National Honor Society, I called the kids at college so they could phone and congratulate him. When Susy was having a rough time with geometry, I asked Chris to talk to her and encourage her. Chris, too, had had a hard time in geometry.

Provide Opportunities for Siblings to Be Together

Encourage them to go out together. Before John left for his first year at college, I said, "Son, I want you to take each of the twins, individually, out to lunch before you leave. I'll finance it, but you do the inviting." I'm so glad I did. Each girl felt special having her big brother all to herself.

Simply running errands or shopping can be a time for two siblings to be together. Both of our boys are color-blind, so it's hard for them to pick out things that match. The twins are flattered when the boys ask them to go with them to find something. They need their little sisters' help!

One more opportunity for them to be together is for a younger sibling to sleep over at college with an older sibling. Allison graduates from college this year, and we've talked about how special it will be for the twins to go down and spend a couple of nights with her and her room-mate before she graduates.

Give Your Children Perspective

We need to remind our kids, especially during the rough times when they dislike each other, that God has given them the exact siblings they need—siblings who will be there for them from birth until death. One day they will like each other. It just takes time—sometimes a long time—for family relationships to heal and to deepen. Meanwhile, God will use the irritating brother or sister in your life in a positive way if you let Him.

My friend Chad, whose sister Kelly often drives him crazy, has seen clearly his difficulty in controlling his temper. He has learned from conflicts with Kelly how much he needs to depend upon God to help him with his temper, and how important it is to learn this while he is still young. It has been difficult, but he has very wise parents who help him see this as a positive learning experience from a long-range perspective.

Love Your Own Siblings

I remember those phone calls. My mother's voice would rise with excitement, and her enthusiasm and joy would permeate the whole house. I could tell exactly who was on the phone. It was one of her brothers.

Mom has two younger brothers, and I grew up knowing that they meant the world to her. Of course, all three kids fought when they were young. She remembers a time when her brother Fitz, who is now a bishop, chased her around the dining room table wanting to kill her. Many of us have experienced this kind of normal frustration with our siblings.

Mom modeled for us kids what it meant to be committed to siblings. She took pride in each of her brothers' accomplishments; she felt pain for their tragedies; she was available whenever they needed her; and she cared for their families. When I was young, we had many family vacations with her brothers and their families. Just watching how they loved each other taught me more about family friendships than any words could have.

They argued about politics and theology and many other things, but they laughed, loved, and always supported each other.

Our children need to see our commitment to our siblings. Model family friendship for your children by calling your brothers and sisters and writing them postcards. Share with your children specific things you admire in your brothers and sisters. Encourage your kids to call their aunts and uncles for advice.

Of course, it is difficult to have any relationship at all with some siblings. Pray for them and take heart from the story of the prodigal son. The prodigal son was also a prodigal brother. Share this story from Luke 15 with your children. Ask them to pray for the sibling who is estranged from you and your family. Ask them to pray for God to show you specific ways to continue loving him, even though you may not see immediate results.

Make a choice. Choose to focus on the positives in your relationships with your own brothers and sisters. A letter to one of your siblings simply sharing your love could be a turning point with your own children for future generations.

Focus Questions

Meditate on Psalm 57.

1. Sometimes when we are dealing with sibling rivalry, we feel like David did in this psalm. How do his words comfort you?
2. How does David's attitude change during the psalm?
3. What aspects of God's character do you most need to focus on today?

Family Friendship Builder

Work together as a family to write a psalm of your own to the Lord.

CHAPTER 11

Friendships Between Parents and Teenagers

All your sons (and daughters) will be taught by the Lord,
And great will be your children's peace.

Isaiah 54:13, parentheses added

Looking out the front window, I noticed our 13-year-old daughter walking slowly down the driveway on her way home from school. Her eight-year-old brother was already home and busily searching in the refrigerator for something to eat.

Opening the front door, I greeted her. "Hey, honey, I'm glad you're home. How was your day?"

"Oooh . . . Okay," she replied in an exasperated voice and threw her backpack on the floor. Making a beeline for the kitchen, she bumped into her brother as he came out.

"Why don't you look where you are going!" She barked with an emphasis that said, *Get out of my way now!*

Casting a quick glance into the refrigerator, she turned accusingly to me. "Why don't we ever have any good food to eat in this house, anyway?"

We did. I had just been to the grocery store that very morning!

Not waiting for an answer, she stomped out and headed to her room, shutting the door with a loud bang that seemed to say, *So there! Everything is all your fault!*

As I stood there in silence trying to figure out what to do, my son looked at me with a puzzled expression on his face and asked, "Mom, what's the matter with Sis?"

"Adolescence, that's what," I replied.

Wonderful and horrible, the best of times and the worst of times, challenging and rewarding—everything you ever heard about the teen years can be true and more. But one word captures the feeling for both parents and adolescents during this season: *awkward.*

Adolescence Is an Awkward Time

The teen years are awkward for our children in several ways:

Physically

Physical changes abound. But these changes don't seem to come at a time or in a way our kids want them. Either they develop too late or too early. For a girl, needing a bra early can be humiliating. Having his voice change late can be agonizing for a boy. You will know your son is sensitive when he puts on a deep voice to answer the telephone. And then there's the pimple. Who ever thought a tiny blemish could be the cause of such despair?

Since hormones are unpredictable, one never knows what mood teens will be in when they walk through the door from school. If Mom is dealing with menopause while her teen's hormones are raging, home can become a challenging place.

Emotionally

Adolescence is an emotionally awkward time. Kids' emotions are fragile. Little things—socks that don't match an outfit, jeans that aren't faded enough, or hair that won't curl properly—tend to be upsetting. Teens are afraid of being embarrassed.

Recently, my 14-year-old got a call late in the evening. She was already asleep when I answered the phone. I told the caller that she had gone to bed. Whoops! That was not the right thing to say. My daughter was humiliated when she learned what I had said.

"How could you have said *that*, Mom? I'm so embarrassed."

I learned and I now say, "I'm sorry she's not available. May I take a message?"

Emotionally, our teens are in two camps. Part of them wants to be a child, whereas the other part desperately wants to be an adult. One minute our daughter wants to curl up in Dad's lap, and the next she insists she doesn't need his advice on improving her time-management skills.

Socially

Teens struggle with social awkwardness. Friends are *very* important during this period of their lives, because they help define who they are. It may seem that the phone is a growth on your daughter's ear, and your son might much rather go out with the guys than come home for family dinner. Sometimes our kids try on different personality types to see what fits best. One day your son may be Mr. Cool, the next a clown or a tough guy. Your daughter may be the friendliest or the silliest, the most talkative or the most organized. It can be exhausting to the family, who's also trying to figure out who this kid is. It's equally frustrating to the child, who isn't sure *who* he wants to be.

Spiritually

The teen years will be an awkward time for your child as he shifts his dependence upon your faith to a more personal dependence upon God. This shift is likely to involve some questioning of his faith as part of the process.

It is not at all uncommon for a maturing teen to think, *Why do I believe what I have been taught?* A necessary spiritual weaning is taking place, and weaning can have some painful moments. But it is crucial that your child believe in God because of his own personal faith.

Parents Feel Awkward, Too

The teen years are not only awkward for our kids, they are also awkward for us as parents. Several things make it awkward.

We Feel Afraid

All of a sudden we feel we don't know what we are doing. Are we making wise decisions? After all, the stakes seem to be higher now. Deciding whether to let a teen go to a particular party seems more crucial than deciding if a six-year-old daughter should take ballet. And all the talk about teenage rebellion! Will our children rebel? We wonder if we really know what our children are thinking. Sometimes it's so hard to get them to talk to us. We fear the unknown. What is really going on in their lives?

We Sense We're Losing Control

We remember those exhausting years of disciplining them as a toddlers. We wondered if we'd live through them. But back then, those toddlers didn't have the persuasive arguments that our teens do. Somehow our reasoning seems out of date. Our arguments don't hold as much weight. Our judgment is questioned.

We struggle with expectations. What is realistic to expect from our teens? What about curfews? What about television and movies? What about time for family? When do we insist and when do we let go?

We Realize They Don't Need Us as Much as Before

We have a growing awareness that we don't have many years left with our teens. We know we must loosen up and let them go, but it's hard. Our job has changed from nurturing to launching, and it's uncomfortable. They are more ready for the launch in some ways than we are, and we are more prepared than they are in others. In their developing maturity, they have begun to recognize some of our weaknesses. This can cause them to feel disloyal. And it can make us feel inadequate.

Yes, the teen years are by definition awkward. Yet, these years can be the most precious time in the life of the child and in the life of the parent. As we begin to let go, we can also begin to cultivate friendships with our teens at a much deeper level. We are moving from a strictly parent-child relationship toward a genuine friendship in which we can share deeply. We can dream dreams together and encourage one another.

Giving Lifelong Gifts to Our Teens

We can give our teenagers *ten gifts* that will enable us to forge strong, life-lasting friendships with them.

1. The Gift of Time

Sixteen-year-old Danny loves to play the guitar. In fact, he plays for the church youth group. Recently, he was in his room trying out some new arrangements on his guitar. As his dad walked by, he poked his head in the bedroom and said, "Hey, son, let me hear some of the things you are playing!"

As Danny began to play for his dad, his father exclaimed, "Why, that's '50s stuff! It's great. I even used to sing that song." For the next hour, loud singing filtered throughout the house as Danny and his dad jammed together, singing and laughing. Later Danny related to a friend that this time of hanging out with his dad was one of his happiest memories.

Hanging out with your kids should be so easy to do, yet it's tough because "more important" things always need your immediate attention. You think, *I'll spend time with my teen when things calm down.* But life doesn't calm down. It only gets more complicated, and before you know it your teen is gone. Hanging out doesn't have to be a big deal or take a lot of time. It can be shooting baskets with a son or daughter for 15 minutes before supper. It might happen when you curl up on the floor of your daughter's room to look through a catalog together. It can happen when your child asks for the car to go to the store. As you give him the keys, ask if you can come along, too. You may get an odd look, but the fact that you simply want to be with your teen with no hidden agenda speaks volumes.

Hanging out is important, and so is participating in planned events. Bill and his teenage son Derek decided to volunteer for a group in our town that feeds the hungry. On many Tuesday nights, you'll find the two of them working side by side in the soup kitchen, serving the needy. Not only are the poor being cared for, but the partnership in caring that this father and son are experiencing is strengthening their bond of friendship.

2. The Gift of Respect

Some time ago, we had a planning meeting in our home with a group of adults. We asked our teenage son John to sit in on the meeting and to give us his feedback. He has a gift of discernment and often he sees things that neither of us do. We really appreciated his help, and our asking for it is a way of showing respect for him and encouraging the development of his gifts.

Study your children. What does this child like to do? What is another one good at? Does a third child have unusual organizational skills? How might we encourage these skills and abilities in each of our children? Every child has gifts, and one of our jobs as parents is to notice and encourage the positive use of those gifts.

Asking our teens' opinions of different things lets them know we are interested in what they think. Their input is valuable and important. We may not agree with our teens' viewpoints, but we respect them as people and we want to hear their ideas. We negate the respect when we feel we must correct their opinions. We must resist this tendency. Their opinions are their own and have great value.

Ask your teenager for some ideas as to how you can be a better parent. It's a scary thing to ask, but if you are prepared simply to listen, you can learn a lot. One dad did this. His teenage son's list included: "Don't put me down in front of my friends"; "Don't begin sentences with 'When I was your age . . . '"; "Don't call me by a pet name in front of my buddies"; "Explain the 'whys' of family policies to me"; "Take me places with you."

Tell your children over and over how proud you are to be their parent. Some people expect teens to be rebellious and difficult even before they are. Some parents groan when they talk about teenagers, even when theirs are great. And some teens feel they have to live up to the bad reputation that's already been given to them before they've done anything wrong.

This past summer my husband and I spoke at a camp about family life. After several days we thought it would be helpful for the parents to hear from some of the teenagers. So we asked our two teenage sons to choose two teenage girls from the camp and form a panel to speak to the parents. One thing the young people told us parents was how important it was to *give teenagers a positive reputation.*

"Stop talking about the teenage years being awful," one requested. "Don't expect your teens to rebel."

"My parents expected me *not* to rebel," another teen commented. "It was not an option. And I haven't."

I have found the teen years to be the most fun of all the child-raising years. Yes, we face struggles and difficulties, but we enjoy blessings as well. If we expect the teen years to be positive rather than negative, we let our kids know that we look forward to, rather than dread, this part of their growing-up experience.

3. *The Gift of Hope*

I remember eighth grade. Oh, how I hated it! I had crooked teeth, thick glasses, was sure I was too fat, and was much taller than the boys. And I wasn't in the "popular crowd." I remember going to my mother in a fit of tears. Throwing her arms around me, she said, "Susan, I remember feeling the same way." Then she told me stories of how she felt when she was my age. Afterward she said, "Your turn will come. You will be pretty and you will have friends." She made me feel normal and she gave me hope. Now my eighth-grade twins love to hear me tell about my miserable junior high years.

Every teen needs a good dose of hope. Because of all the changes and because of the desperate search for approval and acceptance, it is easy for teenagers to despair. They need to know their parents believe in them and are confident their time will come.

The prophet Jeremiah wrote the Jews in exile a letter of encouragement that included: "'For I know the plans I have for you,' declares the Lord, 'plans to prosper you and not to harm you, plans to give you hope and a future'" (Jer. 29:11).

Write out this verse for your teen. Add your personal note that you know God has a very special plan for him. You have confidence in him and you are proud to be his parent.

In your note give your teen a verbal picture of hope for her future. It might go like this:

Honey,

You are unusually sensitive. The positive side of this gift is that you care deeply for people. The painful side is that you are easily hurt. You can sense others' feelings. I know that God is going to use you in a wonderful way to care for people as you grow up. It's a very special gift, and you are a very special young lady.

Occasionally, our teen will run up against a problem that he is sure is going to ruin his life. Things that seem of such acute importance to him now will not be as important given some time and perspective. The daughter who doesn't get invited to the party may be sure she's doomed to being unpopular for the rest of her life. A son who doesn't make the varsity sports team may feel his life is over. A child who worries about not getting into the college of his first choice may feel he's dumb.

What each needs is a loving parent who says, "I know how disappointed you are. But I think you are great, and this probably isn't as devastating as you feel it is right now. Things will get better. Wait and see."

What a teen needs is a reassuring parent who says, "I'm not worried about this. We must do our part and trust the results to God."

When a teen feels shaky about herself, she doesn't need a panicky mom who is equally upset about the issue. She needs empathy and confidence. A good sense of humor and a gift of laughter—if used appropriately—can restore perspective. Often, what we need is a good laugh at our situation. It cuts the tension. Most of all, a teen needs hope—a hope grounded in the knowledge that her parents aren't distressed about her situation, but instead have placed their confidence in an almighty God who is in charge and who loves their child even more than they do.

4. The Gift of Caring for Their Friends

The most significant purchase I have made over the past several years cost $10. I got it secondhand at a garage sale. It's ugly and it takes up room that could be used for something else. It's a source of noise and confusion, frustration and joy. And it keeps me up late at night. It's a Ping-Pong table.

With five kids in their early teens and twenties, I have learned that it is important to do whatever you can to make your house a teen center. Our Ping-Pong table is in the garage; there's no other place to put it. In the summer the big door stays open, and the kids and their friends use the garage as a recreation room. In the winter they play in their coats. In front of the garage is the basketball court, and if they are not playing Ping-Pong, they are probably playing basketball. When the kids are in the garage, they slam doors. When they are on the court, they bounce the ball, shout at each other, and make lots of other noise. Our bedroom is right over this area. My dreams of turning in early faded long ago. But these teen years won't last forever, and I can catch up on my sleep . . . someday.

A Ping-Pong table attracts kids and so does food. My major expense is for groceries. I don't feel so guilty about it when I think of it as an investment in kids' lives.

A third thing that attracts kids is a caring atmosphere. Many times I have wanted to curl up with a book and not visit with the children's friends. Sometimes they wish I *would* disappear. But on the whole I have found it a real encouragement to spend some time visiting with the teenagers.

Recently, my son John said, "Mom, it's important for Joe to come over to visit. He does not get a lot of encouragement from his parents, and he just needs to come over here."

The next time Joe came, I made it a point to ask him about school. Once I asked him to bring a favorite project to show us. I realized then that I had learned some important principles from my son:

Spend time with my friends.
Be interested in them.
Ask them questions.
Draw them out. Care for them.
Cheer for them.

Sometimes it's helpful to ask our children what we should talk about with their friends. We often feel intimidated by teens outside of our own families and don't know what to say to them or how to get them talking to us.

Several weeks ago, we took some of Allison's college buddies out to dinner. During the meal, Allison leaned over and whispered to me, "Mom, ask Mary about her work with the youth group where she's volunteering."

I appreciated my daughter's hint about something to talk about with her friend.

We get to know our children when we spend time with their friends. Go to as many of their events as you can. Drive the car pool. Listen. It's amazing what you learn in automobiles. The kids forget you are there and talk freely. Volunteer to go on field trips when parents are needed.

What do you do if you don't like your child's friends? Be very careful. Spend time getting to know them. Have them in your home. Chances are that either you'll find they aren't as bad as you thought or soon your child will discover a new best friend on his own. Teenagers, especially young ones, change friends frequently. However, if it's obvious that your child's friends are having a negative impact on him, you may need to seek help. Consult a teacher, youth minister, or counselor. In some cases, families have actually moved in order to break the negative influence of a child's peer group.

What if your child doesn't have many close friends? Relax. You may be projecting your need for lots of friends on him. He may be a one-friend-at-a-time person. Some of us need lots of friends, and others gravitate to one or two. We are each different. The bottom line is get to know and try to encourage the people your children spend time with. Loving their friends is a way of building friendships with your own children.

5. The Gift of Parameters

I was almost asleep when I heard whispering in the hall and then an unmistakable bumping sound interspersed with giggles coming from the stairs. *What is going on?* I wondered. I knew John was due in from youth group and Allison had gone to get him. But something was definitely up. It was later than usual, and the bumping and laughter were getting louder. Groggy with sleep, I went out into the hall to see what was happening. Four teens were trying to get the dirtiest-looking couch I had ever seen up the stairs into the boys' room. Now, our two sons are crowded into one bedroom that is nine by 10 feet. There's hardly any unused space.

"What are you doing with that?" I asked.

"Why, Mom, it's our new couch!" John responded joyfully. "I found it on the street during a treasure hunt. Someone put it out for trash, but I thought it would be perfect for our room."

"But it's filthy!" I exclaimed. "Who *knows* what diseases are in it, and it doesn't even have cushions. You can't put that gross thing in your room."

"Mom," my son said in a serious voice, albeit with a twinkle in his eye, "this is my teenage rebellion. Be grateful."

He got me on that, and the couch was moved into an already crowded bedroom where it lived as a monument to his "rebellion" for the next three years. Its presence reminded me of an important principle for parents of teens. Distinguish between basic issues and swing issues.

Teens need parameters and they need freedom. We must carefully choose where to stand firm and where to let go. The couch, though unseemly, was not a basic issue. It was a place to let go. It wasn't vital to character building. It was a place where I could give in, even though my decorator and sanitary instincts did not want to. On the other hand, clear disobedience, back talk, or violating family policies would be issues of the most basic kind where I would have to stand firm.

It's important that Mom and Dad agree on what the crucial issues are for their family. Clear explanation and consistent implementation are vital. Explain the *why* of family policies to your kids. They won't necessarily agree, but it helps your relationship with them if you attempt to explain and to hear their opinions. Then be consistent. "No" means "no" and not "maybe, if you argue enough." A teen sees right through a parent who is wishy-washy, and that parent becomes a "wimp" in the mind of the teen.

We have clearly defined curfews for our teens. They don't go to a home with a member of the opposite sex unless that person's parent is present. And we always know where our kids are and with whom they are spending the evening. If one of them is going to be late or their plans change, they know they must call us. The same goes for us, their parents. We call them when we'll be late. It's family policy.

Our high school kids don't go to movies that have an R rating unless Dad has checked out the movie through someone he respects or has seen it himself. (Our college kids make their own decisions about movies.) Our kids don't watch TV on school nights after the news. The only exceptions might be during basketball season when they want to see a favorite team play, but generally the guideline holds. It's just a Yates family policy. And even though our teens will often argue for more freedom, they do want guidelines. Guidelines communicate to them that we care.

Studies have been easy for our son John. During his junior year in high school, we realized he was making fairly good grades with very little effort and a lack of disciplined study. We wanted him to grow in self-discipline, and we knew he could make top grades with improved study habits. So we instituted a study hall for one quarter. He had to go to a desk in the basement for two hours each day and study something, even if he had no homework. He was not happy with us, but by the end of the quarter his grades had gone up, and he sheepishly said to us, "I really hate to say this, but you were right." The real gift to us was that we watched our son grow in self-discipline. That personal characteristic is benefiting him in a great way as a college student.

When we are firm with our young children, the teen years will be less difficult. Often parents do just the opposite—they are relaxed in the early years and then come down too hard on their children in the teen years. The teen years should have parameters, but there should be a gradual lessening of rules by the parents and the entrusting of self-discipline to the child.

6. The Gift of Flexibility

Yesterday, when I was in the middle of a writing project, my son Chris came in from school and asked if I could take him to the Lincoln Memorial. He needed to write an essay for a creative writing class, and he wanted to do it from the perspective of the statue of Abraham Lincoln. As I hesitated, he said, "Well, maybe I can do it without going down there."

"No," I responded, "I think I could do that. Let's go now."

It hit me that my writing project could wait. I have this son at home for just a year and a half more, and this was an opportunity to spend some time together. I needed to say *yes*. We had a wonderful afternoon together, sharing about each of our writing ventures.

I haven't always been flexible enough to say *yes*. Several weeks ago at bedtime, 14-year-old Susy asked me if I would lie on her bed with her. I frequently do this. It's a great time for special conversations. But this particular night I had bills to pay and I said, "Not tonight, honey. Maybe tomorrow night. I have so much to do."

"Okay, Mommy. I love you," she responded.

Later on, as I thought about her request, I realized what a fool I was. I was so trapped by my schedule and my agenda that I didn't think I could take the time. I now realize that it was much more important to say *yes* to Susy's simple request than it was to pay bills. I had blown it. But I learned a good lesson.

Lord, I prayed, *help me to be more flexible. Help me to become more of a "yes" mother.* Flexibility doesn't conflict with parameters. Instead, the two work together in helping us to be balanced parents. I have to determine once again what the issues are that require rigidity and where I can be flexible.

7. The Gift of Understanding

My friend's son was very upset. His grades had just come, and he had flunked Spanish. It wasn't that he hadn't worked. In fact, he had really tried, but Spanish was just difficult for him. His dad, a successful lawyer, put his arms around his son and said, "Son, I don't know if I ever told you, but I flunked a course in law school."

The gift of understanding was a great comfort to this young man. And the support of his parents in meeting with his teacher and arranging for a tutor helped him improve his grade.

Often, in the midst of a crisis, it might not occur to a teen that his dad or mom once experienced similar failure or embarrassment. It helps to tell our teenagers about the times we have blown it in our own lives.

I asked Libby and Chris on separate occasions, "What do you think teenagers need from their parents?" Chris said *teamwork* and Libby said *partnership*. It interested me that their answers were quite similar and yet they did not know what the other had said. A sense of understanding communicates to our kids that we are on the same team. We pull together in the good times and the bad.

Recently, my husband ate breakfast out with our son Chris. As they visited, John told him about a difficult personnel situation that he felt he had handled badly. He shared some of the lessons he had learned through the experience, and then he asked Chris if he would pray for him to have wisdom in sorting things out.

When we are willing to be vulnerable about our own faults, we will encourage a friendship built on understanding.

8. The Gift of Other Adult Friends

Recently, Allison was home from college. She phoned Doug, a classmate of ours in college and Allison's godfather, to ask him out for lunch. Doug has been a longtime friend, and over the years, he has spent time with her. They have a special relationship. He talks to her about the guy she's dating, what she wants to do when she graduates, and how her faith is growing. He loves her and he asks her good questions.

My friend Holly often has our twins take care of her new baby so she can get some housework done. As she works, she visits with my girls. They discuss friends, school, and other "girl stuff."

Jeff, our youth minister, takes my boys out to lunch. Their conversations have covered sex, priorities, girls, and life decisions. Often, the boys call him for personal advice.

Jeff, Holly, and Doug are having a tremendous impact on our children. They share the same values we do, and they reinforce what we are teaching in our home. Often they give wise counsel to our kids that will be received much better from them than it would be from my husband or me.

Chris received a letter from an adult friend a year ago that was a great encouragement to him. Chris had spoken out in a public meeting about a certain school program. He had taken an unpopular stand. Afterward, a supportive adult named Kay wrote him a note applauding his courage and clarity of thinking on the issue. He still has that note.

Our children need adult role models in their lives other than their parents—adults who will encourage them in their faith, listen to their problems, and reinforce the values that we feel are important.

Invite families to come for a meal. Go on outings with other families. When you are together, spend time getting to know the other family's children. Encourage conversations between your kids and adults. Pray for God to bring into your children's lives some adult mentors. And be available as an adult friend to a child from another family.

When we encourage our children to share our adult friends, we are adding yet another common link to our family friendships—that of shared friends from different generations.

9. The Gift of Loving Our Mates

The greatest thing you can do for your child is to love your child's dad or mom. In a single-parent situation, of course, this is not possible. But for those of us who are married, it may be the most important gift we can give.

Children whose parents love each other are more secure than those who live in distrustful or hateful families. As these fortunate children watch the actions of parents who love each other, they receive lessons in preparing for a healthy marriage themselves.

One youth specialist remarked recently that one of the greatest problems with promiscuity among churched and unchurched teens is that kids think sex equals intimacy. They need to see that intimacy is the outgrowth of a love relationship, and they need to learn that at home.

Do we treasure our mates? Do our kids hear us complimenting them or do we cut them down behind their backs? Do we express affection freely with hugs and kisses? Do we build up each other?

A five-year-old boy was participating in a group where each child was to say something he was thankful for about one of his parents. When his turn came, he said, "I'm glad my dad works so hard to make a living for us." His dad owns his own business and is not at home as much as he would like to be. The boy's mother could be bitter at her husband's long absences, but instead she has communicated a thankful spirit to her children that has been unconsciously picked up by her son.

If we have a mate, we should view them as our greatest treasure. And we should make an effort to welcome single-parent families into our homes. In so doing, we can encourage children of single parents by showing them a picture of what a two-parent family looks like. This gives them a role model for their future marriages. And we need these single parents to help us learn to be sensitive to their needs. In this way, we will become more responsive in caring for others.

10. The Gift of a Consistent Role Model

One family in our city has several boys. Each of the boys has done well in school, has a strong faith, and has a close relationship with his parents. An adult friend asked one what he felt had caused the closeness of their family's relationships and the vitality of their faith.

My young friend responded, "My mom and dad live their faith. We have a simple life-style. We do things together, like scouting."

What strikes me the most about this particular family is the consistency that the son noticed in his parents. Consistency does not mean perfection. We're not perfect. We know it. Our children know it. Yet, they aren't looking for perfect parents, but for honest ones. Our most important role as parents is to live with integrity. We must keep the same standards we set for our kids. Sometimes we will fail. When we are wrong, we need to admit it and ask forgiveness.

Recently, I made a catty remark to my son in front of his date. Later, as I reflected on our conversation, I felt ashamed. I knew I had been wrong and I needed to apologize to my son. I was embarrassed and didn't know exactly what to say. So, I simply said, "Son, I feel that I was insensitive to you, and I shouldn't have said what I did. I'm so sorry, and I need to ask your forgiveness. Will you forgive me?"

Our kids need to see us consistently trying to grow in our relationships with God and in our relationships with one another in the family. As they observe us acknowledging failure and struggling to grow in our faith, two postures will greatly impact their memories: that of us with our arms around our mates, and that of us on our knees in prayer. Holding our mates gives our kids security. Kneeling communicates our humility before God.

We never "arrive" as the perfect parents. Growing in parenting lasts for a lifetime. We are people in process. Frequently, I pray, *Dear God, what do I need to do to be a better parent to these teenagers?* and *Dear God, what would You teach me through these teenagers? I thank You for using these teens in my life, and I thank You that You are the Father of us all.*

Focus Questions

Meditate on Colossians 1:1-14.

1. What do you learn about Paul's love for his friends in these verses?
2. Paul thanks God for specific things about his friends and he prays for specific things for them. What are they?
3. Spend some time thanking God for specific things in your children's lives and then pray for specific needs for them.

Family Friendship Builder

Write out Paul's prayer (verses 9-12), inserting your children's names. Begin to pray this for them and give them copies as gifts of your love.

Write out your family policies with your mate. Then go over them with your teens and post them. Policies might cover subjects such as curfews, movies, television, tithing, chores, family time, and more. For example, children should always let their parents know where they are and whom they are with, and parents should always let their kids know where they are and when they will be home.

It is important for parents to agree on family policies and to clearly communicate them to their children. Get the children's input on some items. Single parents might find it helpful to do this with another couple whose children are close in age to their own.

CHAPTER 12

Friendships Between Parents and Adult Children

Let all who take refuge in you be glad;
let them ever sing for joy.
Spread your protection over them,
that those who love your name may rejoice in you.

Psalm 5:11

I pulled the sheets over my head and snuggled deeper under the down comforter, shutting out the cold, bleak morning. It was already late, and I didn't want to face the day. I knew I had to finish writing a chapter for this book, and I was really struggling with it. I'd been away from writing for a few weeks and in the process had lost my pace. Now I was scared I couldn't get up to speed. I dreaded turning on the computer and so I snuggled down.

Suddenly, the loud ringing of the phone interrupted my misery. It was Allison calling from college. "Mom," she said, "I'm calling just to encourage you. How's your writing coming?"

"Awful," I groaned, and then shared with her my dismal state of mind.

125

"How's *your* writing coming?" I asked, knowing she had two major papers due in three days.

"I'm having a hard time, too," she replied.

After chatting for a few minutes, she prayed for me and I prayed for her. We hung up, both encouraged.

My writing went well that day, but more importantly, my heart soared. All day long I kept thinking, *She's praying for* me. *It was she who called and reached out to me. She understands my frustrations and she encouraged me.*

Over the last few years, a subtle change has taken place in our relationship. As she passes into adulthood, we are becoming peers. My relationship with my daughter has become similar to the friendships I have with my mother and my sister.

Many of us are the parents of adult children, and at the same time, we are the grown children of our parents. Each of these relationships is vitally important. The way in which we relate to our adult children is deeply affected by the relationship we have had and now have with our parents. And each day we live with our children, we are setting patterns for how our adult children will relate to us when we are elderly. In a family, every relationship is intertwined with all the others. That's why building family friendships must involve every relationship within the family.

In this chapter, we will look at our relationships with our adult children. In the next chapter, we will focus on our relationships with our parents and in-laws.

When Do I Become the Parent of an Adult Child?

When do our children pass from adolescence to adulthood? At a specific age? No. The age itself isn't important, but what's happening in the child's life is. We all grow at different rates emotionally, physically, and in every other way. Sometimes the change from child to adult sneaks up on us.

My husband came to me recently and asked in puzzlement, "What happened to the twins? Last summer they were little girls, but now they are young ladies."

"I know," I replied. "They are young ladies now and soon they'll be adults."

He sighed. "But it happened so fast!"

In some ways, young people seem to grow up very quickly, and in other ways, maturity is painfully slow. The season of parenting an adult child will have its own challenges and its own unique blessings. Here are several of the challenges you might face, as well as steps for building upon the blessings.

The Challenge of Relinquishing Control

We must let our children go. This means that an adult child will increasingly make more of his own decisions. Perhaps he decides to buy a couch for his apartment when we feel he should save money for a more reliable car. We might not agree with his choice, but we must let him make it.

The way in which we react to our young adult child's decisions can ease or complicate his period of transition from dependent child to independent adult. For example, when the child was young, we probably gave instructions starting with the words, "You ought to . . . " Now we need to say, "You might consider . . . ," or "Why not think about . . . ?" This is a more effective way to give guidance. The way in which we phrase our thoughts about his decisions is important. The challenge is for us to pray and think before we speak!

But what if our children make poor decisions? They will. So will their parents. It's comforting to remember that our adult children don't answer to us anymore. They now answer to God. Their dependence upon us lessens as their dependence upon their heavenly Father grows.

Letting go is hard for parents, because we realize that our children don't need our input as much or in the same way as they did in the past. We may feel a little left out. Wise parents will understand that their children's independence is healthy. If parents will discover their own new pursuits and new goals rather than hovering over their kids, they will be able to let go more easily.

Relinquishing control should not be a sudden happening. Instead, a slow, steady relinquishing occurs over a number of years. That gives the adult child a sense of easing into adulthood rather than being cast out to swim or sink.

As you relinquish control:

- assume the best of your children;
- give them the benefit of the doubt;
- whenever possible, tell them you have confidence in them; and
- grant them grace when they fail.

The Challenge of Watching Them Make Mistakes

One of the toughest things for parents is to allow their adult children to make mistakes. A friend knew her daughter was skipping classes in a particular course during her junior year in college. Although the child knew attendance was required, she didn't think it really mattered as long as she did the work. And she did all the work. But at the end of the first semester, she received a failing grade in the course because—you guessed it—she had too many class cuts. Her parents had warned her, and her professor had clearly stated the attendance requirements for the class. She had ignored them and now she was in a mess. Would she be able to graduate on time? Her parents had told her they would pay for four years of college, and now she didn't even know if she would be able to finish on time.

Her parents ached to watch her struggle, but they stuck by their four-year commitment and told her she would have to work out the problem on her own. She met with the professor of her failed class, did extensive remedial work, and was finally able to graduate on time.

It was a tough but valuable time for the family. Her dad remarked that the experience was probably one of the best things that happened to her in college, because she learned that *she* was not an exception to the rules. They did apply to her. This experience was a great preparation for life.

It might have been much easier and much less painful in the short term if her parents had assumed she had been unfairly treated or had felt sorry for her and had intervened in her behalf. But in the long run, she would not have learned that all actions have consequences.

Even though watching our kids make mistakes is painful, we must avoid the tendency to cover for them. If we do, we actually enable them to develop poor habits. And they don't get to experience the consequences of their own poor choices in time management, budgetary decisions, and relationship choices. The lessons they learn from their mistakes are valuable tools in teaching them how to live.

The Challenge of Staying Close When They Don't Share Your Faith

Our friends have a son who is in his twenties. Several years ago, these parents discovered a vital relationship with Christ. Their son, however, is a skeptic and does not share his parents' faith. It has been difficult for all of them, because they are a close family. I have learned much from watching these wise parents. Even though their son is not a believer, these parents have continued to share their faith journey with him.

When the father was without a job, he shared his concerns with his son, and he also shared what he was learning about God's tender care during a difficult time. When his mom became ill and fearful, she shared with him how she was having to learn to trust God in a new way. They often ask their son how they can pray for him.

As they talk with their son, they are honest, humble, and never preachy. Through their conversations, they share *something* precious to them—their faith—with *someone* precious to them—their son.

Another thing these parents do is to express interest in their son's interests. When he had a large party in his apartment, they phoned to see how the party went. What food did he serve? Who came and was he pleased with the outcome? When he took a new job in a bank, they learned about the banking business so they could understand his work.

These parents work at developing common interests with their son. His dad asks him to recommend books that he likes so that he can read them, too. He also took up skiing because his son loves to ski.

Because they don't share a common faith, it is especially important for them to work at developing other common interests. These parents want to agree with their son about as many other things as they can. And they are careful to affirm their son in whatever way they can. He knows they are disappointed that he doesn't share their faith, but he has the assurance that they are pleased with him because he is their son.

Recently, his mom put her arms around him and said, "Son, I am so thankful for you. You have always loved your dad and me. You have helped us in so many ways, especially in our bookkeeping. You are gifted about finances. I could never have done what you have, and I am so grateful to you."

These parents also share their adult friends with their son. By including him in special outings with their friends, they are letting everyone know, "This is our son. We are proud of him." Their son is becoming friends with their friends, many of whom are people of deep faith. The love that is being shown him is unconditional, and God will use it in his life to draw him to faith.

Encouraging Friendships with Adult Children

Parenting the adult child is challenging, but it holds rich blessings. The most obvious blessing is that we begin to realize that our children are not only our children but also our dear friends.

Often the transition from teenager to adult is hard. To ease the struggle, we can say, "Honey, I want you to know that the hard time we are having with each other right now is normal. One reason is that you are becoming an adult, and it's awkward. Sometimes you want to be my child and sometimes my peer. It's hard for me, too. Sometimes I don't know if I should be your parent or your friend. But I want you to know that if we stick together and work through this transition time, we have the promise of a beautiful adult friendship."

During this season there are several things we can do to encourage friendships with our adult children.

Set Aside Your Busy Agenda When They Come Home

For days, Joy looked forward to her two daughters coming home. But after the first few days of the phone ringing constantly, the front door banging as friends came and went, and the growing mess in the bathroom, Joy began to wonder, "Why was I so excited about their coming?" Her daily schedule had been interrupted, and her home was no longer orderly. Life seemed tossed upside down.

Many of us can identify with Joy. Her experience is typical. It's helpful to remember that our children's visits home are short, and our times together can be opportunities for furthering our friendships. If we clear our calendars, and set aside our own expectations for what we hope to accomplish, we will be more likely to enjoy these times with our children rather than simply getting through them.

Cancel some of your activities so that you will be available to your children. Take a day's outing together. Have their friends over. On our piano is a photo of a cookout I had with my adult children and their friends. It was a happy and memorable time of building friendships not only with my daughter, but with her friends. Allison and I build memories when we go shopping together. Shopping is not one of my favorite pastimes, but doing it with my daughter makes it fun.

Keep Strengthening Communication

Communication involves talking, listening, and being. Talking is easy, listening can be hard, and simply "being" can be the most difficult for those who are talkers. When a father and his child go hunting, they sit for hours in a blind in silence, waiting for game to appear. There's little verbal communication, but the quiet companionship of a shared experience is valuable in building their friendship.

To be a good listener, we need to learn to ask specific questions. All too often our questions are too general and require a one-word answer.

"How was your semester?"

"Fine."

Not a lot of in-depth sharing results from general questions. On the other hand, the following questions may spark a deeper conversation.

"What classes have you enjoyed the most this year? Why?"

"What has been the biggest surprise you have faced in your new job?"

"What new person have you most enjoyed getting to know? What do you enjoy about him?"

When we relax our own personal schedules and are available to our adult children, we create an atmosphere that encourages communication.

Ask Their Advice

One blessing of having adult children is that now we find ourselves asking *them* for advice. John and I were trying to decide between two different camps for the twins to attend during vacation. We honestly could not decide which was best for them. Since our older kids had been to both camps, it was natural to go to them for advice. Not only did they have the experience, but they also understood the twins' needs, and the older kids' perspective enabled them to advise us.

Remember, each family member has unique gifts. As our children become adults, these gifts become more developed. Perhaps a child is clever with figures and financial planning. Ask for advice on how to make a budget and stick to it. Another may have a good eye for decorating. Ask for help in redoing a room. Every time we ask our children's advice, we are encouraging peer friendships with them.

Share Your Life with Them

Relationships are two-way. Sharing is not only about parents finding out how our children are doing, it's also about sharing our lives with them. Now our conversations and relationships are more adult to adult. The sharing is more personal and deeper—more intimate and vulnerable.

Recently, Allison became engaged. We are so excited because her fiancé, Will, is clearly the answer to our prayers for our daughter. It's a new season for us as we approach the first wedding of one of our kids. And it's a bit scary. I've begun to think for the first time about being a mother-in-law.

When we began to make wedding plans, I sensed some tension in the air. The feeling wasn't specific—just an uneasiness on my part. And I wanted so much for the planning to be a special experience for Allison and me. Finally, I went to Allison and, throwing my arms around her, said, "Allison, I don't know what I'm doing. You're our first child to be married and it's scary for me. I do so want to be a good mother and mother-in-law for Will. And I want all this planning to be fun. But you'll have to help me and promise to tell me if I get too pushy. We'll have to learn together."

Our children need to know that we sometimes feel awkward and unsure. When we share our fears honestly with them, our relationships become more peer to peer. Sharing our needs, and asking our adult children to pray for us, becomes a "welcome mat" to a mature friendship.

Stay in Touch When They Are Away

As I mentioned earlier, one of the biggest items in our budget is our long-distance phone bill. The phone can be a nuisance, or it can build friendships. Encourage your children to phone you and one another.

But don't limit communication to the telephone. You can't save phone calls, but you can save letters. Some of my most precious treasures are letters I received from my parents. Letters can be read over and over, and they can offer continual encouragement.

After my father-in-law died unexpectedly, my brother-in-law was cleaning out his office desk. In the top drawer, he found a well-worn letter written by my husband when he was a student in graduate school. In the letter, my husband told his dad how much he appreciated him and how he felt that he had not communicated it in the way he wanted.

The frayed letter in the top drawer of a busy executive indicated he valued it very much. The discovery of it upon the death of his father greatly comforted John. He still has it today.

A friend of ours has two married daughters. Each month he sends them his wife's and his own schedules. Bible studies, doctor appointments, social engagements—everything is on it. This is his way of keeping his adult children informed about their parents' lives. It's connecting.

Our refrigerator holds a mess of notes and pictures. Stuck in a prominent place among the stuff are two pieces of paper with a weekly schedule written out. Our collegians, John and Allison, make these schedules for us each semester. When I'm in the kitchen during the day, I can look at their schedules and see what they are doing. John is in Greek class on Mondays and Wednesdays at 9 A.M. I'm reminded to pray for him. It's a tough course. Allison has a sorority meeting on Sunday nights. I'm reminded to pray for her sorority sisters. These schedules help me feel in touch when the kids are away.

A father shared with me a letter he received from his daughter, who was teaching English in Japan for a summer:

Dear Daddy,

The reason I'm writing you this note is to thank you for working where you work and doing what you do. Because you go to that frustrating office every day, I get to be here and grow spiritually and in every other way. You have enabled me and the boys to find our gifts and to use them. You and Mama have challenged me to set goals and have shown me how to reach them. You've taught me what it means to follow through. Your example has been great. Who knows whom I'll marry? I just hope he has many of the same qualities you have.

I love you,
Your daughter

In this letter, we glimpse a precious friendship between a father and his adult daughter—a friendship that is possible for you, too. You may think a friendship between you and your adult child can never happen in your family, but Jesus Himself has said, "With God all things are possible" (Matt. 19:26).

Focus Questions

Meditate on Titus 2:1-8.

1. Make a list of things mentioned here that you are to teach your adult children.
2. What should your attitude be as you teach?
3. What quality do you need help on in your own life?

Family Friendship Builder

Get together with some parents whose children are older than yours and who have good relationships with them. Ask them how they developed close bonds with their adult children. Take notes on what they say. Pray for your friendships to grow with your adult children.

PART FOUR

Forging Bonds
Between Generations

Strengthening Friendships with Parents and In-Laws

Listen to me . . .
you whom I have upheld since you were conceived,
and have carried since your birth.
Even to your old age and gray hairs I am he,
I am he who will sustain you. I have made you and I will carry you;
I will sustain you and I will rescue you.

Isaiah 46:3, 4

*M*y friend really had a problem. In fact, she was overwhelmed with tears of anxiety as she poured out her frustrations. "Susan," she said, "you know how I have struggled with my relationships with my mother and in-laws. The saving factor has been that we don't live in the same town with them. But now my husband has been offered a great job in the town where they all live. I don't know what we should do! If we move there, my in-laws will want us to spend every moment with them. Our values are so different. They spoil our kids and give our son candy even though he's allergic to it. We've explained his medical problem to them, but they continue to give it to him.

"My mother, who also lives there, is old and alone, and she will expect and need our attention. She makes me feel guilty if I go to my in-laws' house. I'm afraid the tension our parents may cause will affect our own marriage. I want to have a good relationship with all of our parents, but I feel pulled apart by them. And no matter what I do, I can't seem to please everyone."

My friend's problem is all too common. How can we build strong relationships with our parents and our in-laws? What do we do when we disagree about crucial issues? Can we please our mates and our parents at the same time? And how do we pave the way for good relationships between grandparents and grandchildren? Hard questions. No simple answers. And yet we can do some positive things to strengthen these important friendships.

My husband planted a small azalea bush in our garden. He carefully dug the hole deep enough for the plant to be secure so it wouldn't topple over when knocked by dogs and running children. And the soil needed to be well prepared with nutrients and water. A deep hole and prepared soil provide the essential foundation from which the fragile plant can develop into a healthy bush bursting with pink blossoms.

In a similar way, two essential principles are needed to provide us with a healthy foundation from which to develop friendships with our parents and in-laws.

First, if we are married, we must agree with our mates concerning what is best for our own families. Second, we must do all we can to honor our parents. Sometimes a parent can drive a wedge between married people. This must not happen.

When Ellen married Ray, she knew his mother was a strong woman. But she wasn't prepared for her constant influence in their lives. She *expected* to be phoned several times a week. She dictated how they should spend their holidays, where they should go on vacation, and how Ray should spend his annual bonus. One evening when Ellen was struggling with her job and trying to talk to Ray, his mom called and wanted him to come over to help her with something. As Ray said, "Yes, Mother," and hung up the phone, Ellen burst into tears.

"I need you tonight, Ray. You always put your mother first. She runs our lives. I'm your family now. And I need you."

Although his wife was upset, Ray knew there was truth in what she said. He felt caught between two women, unable to please either. Fortunately, Ray had a strong faith from which he had developed a clear sense of priorities. He knew he had to put his wife first. It was not easy, but he began to live that way. The next time his mother wanted him to do something, he said, "Mom, let me check on some things and I will call you back." And he discussed her requests with Ellen. Often he had to make painful choices, and many times his mother did not understand. But because he had a clear sense that his wife (and later their kids) came first, his marriage grew, and Ellen, feeling secure in her position, began to work *with* him to care for his mother. She soon realized there were times in which she needed to take a backseat and let Ray care for his mother first. Several years have passed and still there are rough times, but the marriage has been strengthened as Ellen and Ray have sought to put each other first and then to honor his mother.

The fifth commandment says, "Honor your father and mother, so that you may live long . . . " (Ex. 20:12).

We are admonished to honor our parents. If we are single, our responsibility is to our own parents; but if we are married, our responsibility is not only to our parents, but to our in-laws as well. It is true that when we marry, we marry a family. Part of becoming one in marriage involves the sharing of all things, and that includes our parents.

The great Bible story of Ruth and Naomi illustrates for us a tender example of honoring one's mother-in-law. Facing a famine in Judah, Naomi fled with her husband and two sons to the country of Moab. There they raised their sons and saw them married to Moabite women. When her husband and both sons died, Naomi decided to return to her native country of Judah. Although she encouraged her daughters-in-law to remain in their own country, Ruth chose to go with her, saying: "Where you go, I will go, and where you stay, I will stay. Your people shall be my people and your God my God" (Ruth 1:16, 17).

Ruth's faithfulness to her mother-in-law resulted in her marriage to one of Naomi's kinsmen and having the honor of being the great-grandmother of King David and a direct ancestor of Jesus, the Messiah.

My neighbor Edith died this year at the age of 87. For the past two years, she has been completely bedridden. Her three adult children have taken turns caring for her in her home. They have had to make many personal sacrifices to do this, but they have done it, not with resentment, but with a real sense of joy. Why and how?

A glance back into their own childhood offers some clues. When Edith was a young mother with three children, they lived in a small row house. Edith's father suffered a stroke; soon afterward, her mother had a breakdown. Edith's mother was unable to care for her father, so Edith and her husband moved her sick parents into their small three-bedroom home. A little later, when Edith's mother-in-law was diagnosed with cancer, they brought her to live with them so they could care for her as well. Three sick parents and three small children! I don't know how she did it. I only know that she had a strong faith and a gentle spirit. She lived out what it meant to honor her parents. Is it surprising that her own children would spend two years caring for her?

If we want our children to honor us, they must first see us honoring our own parents.

God has called us to serve our mates and to honor our parents. These two foundational principles are vital in building friendships within the family. It will not always be easy. It may be inconvenient and costly to honor your parents. And you will not be able to please everyone. Your ultimate job is not to keep everyone happy, but to be faithful to God's calling, which is to love your spouse, to nurture your children, and to care for your parents.

With a solid foundation in place, our azalea bush can begin to grow. It will need continued gentle nurturing to blossom into a beautiful plant. Our family friendships need gentle nurturing, too.

Six Ways to Nurture Friendships with Parents and In-Laws

1. Expand the Positives

If we asked ourselves, "Whose approval do I most desire?" our parents and in-laws would rank somewhere near the top of the list. We want our parents to be proud of us, and we long for their approval. This desire can cause us to be overly sensitive to them, especially in the beginning of a new season of life.

As a newlywed, you decide to change your hairstyle. Your close friend says she thinks it looks best long. You take that as good advice. But if your mother-in-law says she'd like it long, you take it as interfering. Or, your toddler is misbehaving and your good friend says he needs a "time-out." You may welcome her insights, but if your mother had been the one to say that, you might have taken it as criticism of your parenting skills: "How can she be so critical?" Or, you work hard to clean your house before your folks come over. They fail to comment on how lovely it looks, so you assume they are displeased.

It's so easy to overreact or to give too much weight to our parents' comments or lack of comments. Becoming critical of their responses, we begin to dwell on the negatives when we ought to expand the positives. Even if there are genuine problems, we have to decide whether we are going to focus on the disappointments or choose to accentuate the positives.

It's helpful to ask, *Is my attitude toward my parents positive or negative?* Our attitudes will be communicated by how we live and what we say, and our children will pick up on them. The following stories illustrate two different attitudes.

A couple has a difficult relationship with the husband's parents. His parents rarely spend time with their grandchildren and they are often critical. Their way of communicating is to give money. The young father is full of bitterness and hurt and often complains about his parents in front of his kids. At a young age, his children are already developing a negative spirit toward their grandparents. As they sit at the dinner table and hear their mom and dad complain, these kids are learning how to treat parents. When they grow up, what will they say at *their* dinner table about *their* parents?

In another home, the young parents also have a difficult relationship with the husband's mother. She is overly critical of her adult son. He can't seem to please her, and it would be easy for him to speak badly about her in front of his kids. But he has chosen to focus on the positives. He looks for good things about his mom to tell his children. He points out how kind it was of her to come visit, even though she is very busy. When he needs to, he gently tells the children that they must love and forgive her when she says things she shouldn't. And he seeks to thank and praise her whenever he can. When his kids grow up, will they be likely to forgive him when he's cranky and insensitive? Do you think they will point out his *faults* or his *strengths* to their children?

We may not be aware of what we are communicating to our kids about our parents, but as they see us relating to our parents, they are learning how to treat us when *we* become elderly parents. We must make the choice to look for the good and pass along that attitude to our children.

2. Learn from Them
No matter what our parents are like, they possess two things that we

don't—age and experience. With age comes experience and wisdom. And the older one becomes, the longer he has had to develop personal gifts and talents. Each of us can learn from our parents. They have lived a life different from ours, in a world different from ours.

We can ask ourselves several questions about our parents:

"What are their gifts?"
"Do they have wisdom?"
"Do they do something well?"
"Do they have a unique talent they could teach us?"

Some time ago, my husband, John, was struggling with a personnel problem in his office. He was really stuck and did not know how to handle the potentially explosive situation. He desperately needed wisdom and felt that he didn't have much! So he picked up the phone and called my mother. This was perfectly natural, because one of my mother's gifts is wisdom. She has had much experience with people, and she has an unusual ability to see clearly in the midst of a mess. She listened and was able to give my husband several insights that helped him decide what to do. It was mutually beneficial. He was helped by her insights and she was encouraged by being needed. And their friendship grew a little deeper because of his trust in her judgment.

My friend Frank realized that his dad had an uncanny knack for numbers. He was also wise about financial matters. Newly married, Frank needed some advice on investments, debt, and savings. So he asked his dad how he kept records and what advice he could give him. Pulling out his well-worn record book, Dad showed him pages of computations and gave him sound advice. Each time Frank went home to visit, they got out the faded record book and his dad showed him how different investments were doing. Their times together with the old record book became a tradition, and a special bond grew between the two men—all because a young man asked his dad to teach him something.

One specific thing we can learn from our parents is a sense of history. My grandmother grew up on a plantation in the Deep South. She remembers her parents talking of things that happened to their family during the Civil War. Before Granny's health failed, our children interviewed her on tape. They asked questions like:

"What had been invented by the time you were a child?"
"What was your school like?"

"What work did your parents do?"

"What individuals and events had an impact on your life? Why?"

"How did your faith in God develop?"

Granny described for us what it was like to see her first car, and she told fascinating stories of a life without televisions or computers. To our kids, her descriptions were of another world, and the stories she told made history and sociology come alive! Each of our kids has a copy of the tape, and Granny's stories will one day be played for their children, giving them a sense not only of American history but of family history as well.

3. Initiate Activities and Show Thoughtfulness

It's so easy to expect our parents to initiate activities with us. After all, they are our parents. We've grown up responding to them. So we wait, longing to spend time with them and wondering if and when they'll make a move toward us. Could it be that they need *us* to reach out to *them*? Yes. We can't expect our parents to continually take the initiative for getting together with us.

Jodie has had a difficult relationship with her dad, and yet she longs to grow closer to him. As we chatted one day, I asked her, "What does your dad like to do?"

After thinking for a moment, she replied, "Well, he often takes walks."

"Ask him if you could join him for a walk," I suggested. "Go with him with no agenda other than to enjoy being with him. And go as often as you can. It may feel awkward at first, but if you persist, you'll be surprised at how much more comfortable you both will become. Walks are 'his thing,' and you need to go where *he* is comfortable. You'll be amazed how a simple gesture like a walk can open the doors to a deeper relationship."

How can we show thoughtfulness to our parents? We can:

WRITE TO THEM. Write to your in-laws to thank them for having and raising your mate. Thank them for all the nights they took care of him when, as a baby, he kept them awake. Thank them specifically by telling them the qualities you most appreciate in your mate.

PHONE THEM. As we've already mentioned, use the phone to build relationships. Call your parents often. Don't expect them to be the ones to phone you. Reach out to them. If they have an answering machine, leave love messages. If they have a fax machine, send notes. It's easy to communicate when there is something urgent to discuss, but the most meaningful communications occur when we simply say, "I called for no reason other than to say I'm thinking about you today and I wanted you to know I love you."

VISIT THEM. My friends in the story at the beginning of the chapter had a problem. If they moved, she feared their parents would expect frequent visits, would be jealous of each other, and would not appreciate that she and her husband needed time alone with their children—without grandparents. My friend and her husband solved the problem when they sat down together and agreed on a reasonable compromise. They drew up a tentative plan for when they would eat meals with one or the other set of their parents and what times they would reserve for their own family. Then they informed their parents. The plan wasn't met with a lot of enthusiasm, but they were united as a couple, and over time, their parents accepted the plan.

My friends worked hard at making the time they spent with parents special. Naturally, they had to be flexible as needs arose, but because they generally stuck to their plan, they were able to be gracious when unique situations occurred.

We need to visit our parents as often as is reasonably possible, and we need to invite them to visit us as well.

CELEBRATE WITH THEM. My cousin's dad was in failing health. Over the years my cousin had not been able to spend much time with him. He had been away at school and then abroad with the military. Now he longed to have some time while his dad could still enjoy being with him. He thought about what his dad would like and realized he would love a trip back to the state where he grew up. So my cousin took time off from work, made the arrangements, picked up his father, and together they made a journey back to their roots. It was a tender celebration of a sick father and his adult son walking through old streets, sharing memories.

4. *Care for Them When They Are Old and Ill*

How you do this will vary with your circumstances. As we remember our two essentials—consider what is best for your own family, and consider how to honor your parents—it is helpful to:

ASSESS THE SITUATION. What are their needs? Where do you live in relation to them? What extended-family support is available? What resources such as financial, health care, housing, etc., are available? (A broader checklist is included at the end of the chapter.)

Then, consider the needs of your immediate family. If you are struggling with toddlers or both husband and wife are working in careers with little flexibility, your options will be limited. If you are single or do not have children, you may be in a better position to help.

Communicate clearly with your extended family as you make decisions about your aging parents. Working together to solve problems could become an opportunity for brothers and sisters to deepen their friendships.

BE WILLING TO MAKE HARD DECISIONS ABOUT THEIR CARE. Encourage your parents to make their own choices as long as they can, but realize that the time may come when you must step in and begin to make some decisions for them. You must be willing to decide what is medically and practically best for them even if they don't agree. And they may not like the decisions. They may think they can still drive a car or live alone when they truly cannot. You may have to intervene for their safety and the safety of others, and they may not like it.

It's helpful to call a family conference with your siblings to discuss your parents' needs and the options for their care. Be willing to do research to determine what help is available. Then, present some simple options from which your parents can choose. Simplifying complex issues into manageable options helps when dealing with the elderly. And by simplifying the issues, you can focus on them more clearly. If you take time to research and plan ahead, the stress of making difficult choices will be lessened.

BE WILLING TO MAKE PERSONAL SACRIFICES. You must be willing to sacrifice time, space in your home, and financial resources to care for your parents. It won't be easy. Caring for older parents can be inconvenient and time-consuming. But just remember, you weren't easy to care for as their baby. You were hard to raise and often exasperating. You demanded sacrifice. Now it is your turn to honor them and sacrifice for them.

Caring for our parents can be a wonderful time of growth for us personally. Remember, God will not call us to do something without giving us the personal resources to do it. As we are faithful to His calling, we will be richly blessed.

5. Maintain a Sense of Humor

Sometimes we feel like the children and our parents feel like our parents. Then, suddenly, they act like children and we feel like the parents. The relationship has turned upside down and it feels very strange. It's difficult to find oneself parenting parents.

Trish is a single parent in her fifties. Her daughter, Wendy, is 27 and lives with her. One evening Trish went with a blind date to the theater. She expected to return home right after the show, but she and her date were having such a good time, they went out for a late dinner. When she opened the front door, it was 1 A.M. Suddenly the hall light came on, and there stood a very sleepy, very concerned daughter.

"Mother," she exclaimed, "where have you been? You are later than you said you would be. And I didn't know anything about your date. You could have been in real trouble. I was about to call the police."

As Trish stood on the steps, she experienced a sudden flashback of herself in the same position years earlier! After Trish apologized to her daughter for causing concern, the two had a good laugh about their role reversals.

Sally's mother is 90. All of her life, Sally has looked up to her mother. Now, in her older years, her mother has begun to have temper tantrums, and often Sally feels like she is dealing with a toddler instead of a mother. It's so out of character, and both of them feel uncomfortable.

When we experience an awkward time in our relationships with our older parents, it is comforting to realize we are not alone. Others are having similar experiences. In this season, it's helpful to look for the humor.

Barbara's mother is 98. For years she has lived with Barbara, who is single, in Barbara's apartment. Nursing help enables Barbara to care for her mother at home. Recently, however, her mother told Barbara she was thinking of moving out.

"Why, Mother?" Barbara asked. "Aren't you happy with the care here?"

"It's not the care," her mother responded. "It's just that I'd like to be with some men!"

6. Prepare for "No Regrets"

When our parents and in-laws die, we want to look back with a sense of gratitude rather than a feeling of regret. "But you don't know how bad my relationship with my parents has been," you might respond.

That's right. I don't know . . . but God does. And He has been there with you even in the most painful times. No matter how difficult your family relationships were, you must believe that your parents did the best they could, given what they themselves came from. Hardly any parent sets out to do a bad job of raising his own children. The good news is that it is never too late to do what is right, to get things straightened out, to ask for forgiveness, and to start over.

Pat was raised in an abusive home. Her only brother adopted the gay life-style, and she became estranged from her father. Recently, her brother was diagnosed with AIDS. The same week her father was told that he had terminal cancer. Pat longed to minister to both her brother and father, but she knew that in her father's case, she needed to forgive him before she could help him. It was painful and difficult, but with God's tender mercy she forgave her dad, and just before he died, he gave his life to Christ and asked for His forgiveness.

Then as she nursed her brother in his final days, he too surrendered his life to a loving heavenly Father who understands pain and who is able to forgive and restore relationships.

Pat's story is one of gratitude for relationships redeemed instead of regret and bitterness for relationships lost. Each of us must do all we can to live with "no regrets." We don't know what the future holds, and we don't want to look back and say, "I didn't get to tell him I was sorry," or "I wish I had told her I loved her."

Sometimes it's helpful to look ahead and ask ourselves, "How will I look back on this time in a few years?" We may realize that we need to forgive or to ask for forgiveness, we may need to write a letter expressing love, or we may need to give the gift of our time to sit with a parent who is ill. Whatever we must do, we should do it *now*, for we may not have as much time left as we think we do.

When my dad died unexpectedly, I was devastated. He was so healthy, so alive, so young. I didn't expect his death when it happened. In my grief, I thought about our relationship and I wept. I wept because I had been blessed with a truly great father. And I wept because I wondered if he knew how much I loved him.

My mother's most comforting comment to me was, "Susan, your daddy never doubted how much you loved him. He knew. He really knew." Even now when I think about him, I say to myself, *He knew! He knew!* and the tears flow; but they are tears of gratitude, not regret.

Focus Questions

Meditate on the Book of Ruth.

1. Describe different aspects of Naomi and Ruth's relationship.

2. What specific ways did they care for each other?
3. Ask God to show you needs that your parents or in-laws have. Pray for them and take at least one step to express your care for them this week.

Family Friendship Builder

As a family, seek out some elderly person to care for. For example, visit a neighbor, offer to take an older person on an errand, or take your children to a nursing home to visit the residents. Expose your young children to the elderly. If you do, your kids will grow up to be more comfortable caring for the aged.

Another activity that will help build relationships is to use the following worksheet to explore care for your parents and in-laws.

Caring for Our Parents and In-Laws

As we seek to honor and care for our aging parents, we need to assess three areas.

Housing and Logistics
1. Is their living situation adequate for now? Is it necessary to add conveniences or services to allow parents to age in their current place? (For example: yard work, maintenance, housekeeping, driving substitutes.)
2. Is their home adaptable for future years? (For example: there is a first-floor bedroom and bath; the house is accessible from the outside without steps.)
3. What are their wishes about housing and care should they become incapacitated? Have they considered the local options or looked at any continuing-care communities?
4. Is there a need for assistance or simplification regarding grocery shopping and making meals? Consider Meals-on-Wheels, individual frozen dinners, microwave meals, or other creative support systems to allow elderly parents to stay independent.
5. Is it still safe for them to be driving? A family doctor may be able to help decide if they are still capable of driving.

Financial and Legal
1. Are they managing their finances adequately? Can you help with writing checks, arranging automatic deposit, or having their bills sent to you instead of to them?

2. Is there an inventory of assets, including insurance policies and retirement plans? Is property held jointly with others? Who are the beneficiaries on the policies?

3. Have they had legal counsel on drawing up an estate plan? (This is crucial for estates over $600,000.) Is their attorney a member of the National Association of Elder Law Attorneys?[1]

4. Are essential documents prepared and available as needed? These documents should include durable, general power of attorney, advance directives for health care, and a will.

5. Does someone know the location of their safety deposit box and key, and do they have documents stored in other places?

Spiritual
While we prepare financially and legally for death, it's even more important to prepare spiritually. Take the opportunity to share with your parents how much God loves them. Give them specific scriptures. Review the basics of a personal relationship with Christ, including His forgiveness and the assurance of eternal life with Him that we have as believers. If you do this in writing, your parents can read and reread and reflect on the message more often than if it is shared only in conversation.[2]

CHAPTER 14

Forging Bonds Between Grandparents and Grandchildren

Children's children are a crown to the aged,
and parents are the pride of their children.
Proverbs 17:6

S he's almost 87. Her white hair is wrapped neatly into a bun and fastened at the nape of her neck. Her porcelain skin is beset with the wrinkles of age. The pain of a crushed vertebra causes her to walk slowly, but it has not hindered her spirit. When you first meet her, you notice her immaculate clothing and carefully applied makeup. But as you gaze at her face, it's her deep blue eyes that overwhelm you. Alive with a sparkle, they draw you in as if to say, "Tell me about yourself. I want to know you."

When I asked why this woman was so special, one of her 15 grandchildren told me, "She has always been genuinely interested in me. I remember when my cousin and I once went to visit her. We got into our nightgowns and curled up on her bed about nine o'clock, and we talked until after midnight. That night Grandma Monie asked questions like, 'Are a lot of girls at your college sleeping with their boyfriends?' Can you imagine an 87-year-old asking that? But one of the neatest things about Grandma Monie is that she asks good questions. She's interested in our generation. She wants to know what we think, what our friends think and do, and what challenges we face. And she encourages us by looking for the good in us and by building us up. I always have to laugh when she compliments me on my eyebrows. She says they are shaped so beautifully. Who else would ever notice the shape of someone's eyebrows?

"Grandma Monie has even given us flirting lessons. She tells us to find out what a boy is interested in and then ask him questions about his sport or hobby. 'Act like he's the most fascinating man you've ever met,' she says. Her sense of humor makes it fun to be with her. And she is wise," the young woman concluded.

Another of Monie's granddaughters said, "I feel I can share anything with her, and she will offer her perspective and her advice. Most of all, I know she prays for me. Many times when I have most needed it, she has put her arms around me and prayed for whatever was on my mind. I know that she prays for each of us grandchildren every day."

For this great lady, being a grandmother is a joy. Her life demonstrates it and her grandchildren know it. And being a grandparent can be a joy for you as well. Grandparents get to do all those things they didn't have time to do with their own kids because they were too tired, too stressed, too overwhelmed. Grandparenting is fun, because it is not usually a 24-hour-a-day job. You get to return the kids at the end of the day!

Being a grandparent isn't limited to being a biological grandparent. Some children don't have any living grandparents. Others live far away from theirs. And some older folks never had children of their own. Yet they can be "grandparents," too. Anyone can be a grandparent whether single or married, with or without kids. Young parents and their children need the influence and example of older people in their lives.

For several years, we lived across the street from Alf and Marjory. Australian in background, they had spent more than 25 years ministering in Africa before they retired. Now in their sixties, they had come out of retirement to help start a new evangelical seminary in a new country. They had never had children of their own and yet, to our children and to many others, they were grandparents. It was not unusual for Alf to wander over late in the afternoon and get down on the floor to play Legos with our two-year-old. With our own parents living far away, John and I looked to Alf and Marjory for wisdom and encouragement. Even though we no longer live near them, their impact on our lives continues. We often find ourselves saying, "What would Alf and Marjory do?"

Whether our grandparents are biological ones or adopted like Alf and Marjory, we parents will play an important role in determining the relationships our children and their grandparents will have.

The Parents' Role

Parents are the main link between grandparents and grandchildren. We have three responsibilities to carry out as we seek to nurture these special relationships. We need to:

- pave the way for positive relationships;
- act as the interpreter between generations; and
- help them find time to be together.

Parents Pave the Way for Positive Relationships

We've already seen how important it is to honor our parents. The reality of what it means to honor a parent becomes apparent as we pave the way for our children to have a positive relationship with them. What we *say* about our parents will greatly influence what our children *think* about them.

A young mother says to her son, "Your grandfather is so reliable. I can always count on him. And Grandmother has such a wonderful sense of humor. She makes me laugh." Small positive statements like this will reap big dividends in the mind of a child.

But what if there are problems with your parents? Be honest with your children. Don't try to hide the difficulties.

Sara had an unpleasant mother-in-law. And the older her mother-in-law became, the more unpleasant she was. The whole family knew she was a grouch. Sara didn't pretend the older woman was wonderful. Instead, she said to her children, "Yes, Grandma is unpleasant, but she's still your grandmother. We must keep loving her. I know it's hard, but let's think about how we can do it."

Wisely, Sara learned to laugh about Grandma's peculiarities instead of taking them too seriously. And her children developed a lighthearted rather than critical spirit about their grandmother.

If a grandparent has a severe problem such as alcoholism or mental instability, or has a history of abusive behavior, we must protect our kids from harm. But even then we can choose to focus on good qualities in them rather than pointing out the negative ones. We need to encourage our children to pray for them, no matter what.

Equally important as what we say about our parents is how we treat them. We sometimes take advantage of our parents by expecting them to do all our baby-sitting and, in other ways, to be at our beck and call. We must keep in mind that they have already invested many years caring for children. We must not expect them to be on call for us. We must be sensitive to their needs. They need a life of their own.

We will know what grandparents' needs are as we keep communication honest and open. Grandmother needs the freedom to say, "I'm just not up to baby-sitting." Honor her when she feels this way and be gracious. Grandfather needs to be able to say, "I don't feel like going fishing right now." You need to help your kids accept this.

Our children will learn much about relating to their grandparents by watching us relate to them. But they won't get everything they need to know by observation. We must *train* them to honor their grandparents. We must *teach* them to be respectful and thoughtful.

Make sure your children speak with respect. Discipline them if they do not. Instill in them good manners. "Hold the door for your grandmother. Stand up when she enters the room. Offer her your chair."

Teach your kids to thoughtfully care for their grandparents. Remember their birthdays and Grandparents' Day. Small children can make cards; older kids can call or send a card or gift.

Have your kids write thank-you notes when grandparents have done something special for them. Give the kids a deadline. If necessary, withhold privileges until the notes are written. If you read Ann Landers' column, you will notice that her letters most often fall into two categories: letters from people in pain over affairs and letters from grandparents in pain because they never receive thank-you notes from their grandchildren. If we train our kids when they are young, they will probably continue the habit when they are grown.

Ask your teenagers to phone and write their grandparents. "But I don't know what to say," they may reply.

"Just tell them what's going on in your life, about your classes, your friends, what papers you are working on. Grandma needs to feel included in your life. She cares about you." Teenagers probably won't take the initiative to write or call; they need to be reminded.

Parents Interpret Between Generations

Our children's first knowledge of their grandparents comes through us. And grandparents will get to know the children through us as well. In a sense, we act as interpreters.

Once again, as you do in interpreting the actions of one sibling to another, it's helpful to use the "clue in" principle for grandparents and grandchildren.

What are your child's interests? Clue in Grandpa about those interests. Tell him that at this particular moment trains are "hot" for your small son. Suggest Grandpa cut train pictures out of magazines and mail them to his grandson. Then, when the pictures arrive, help your child make a homemade scrapbook for Grandpa's trains.

Don't expect your parents to guess what your child likes. They are at a disadvantage because they don't know your child as well as you do. Just clue them in and make life easier for everyone. But be careful how you do it. "I sure wish you'd read to the kids sometime," could be interpreted, "You don't do much with my children."

It might be better to say, "You know what would really thrill the kids? If you would read them this book. It's their favorite, and it would be very special if you would read it to them."

If you have teenagers, suggest to grandparents what they can talk about with them. Is your son a reader? Tell Grandma some of the books he's interested in so she can ask him about them. Is a daughter playing tennis? Let Grandpa know so he can inquire about her games.

Sometimes grandparents will do something that is *not* helpful and can even be *dangerous*. The friend I told about in the last chapter asked her in-laws not to give her son candy because he is allergic to it. His grandparents' motive was to build a relationship, but they were approaching it the wrong way. The parents needed to make sure the boy's grandparents understood why he could not have candy.

If you are having a similar problem, first explain the problem to the grandparents and then purchase a favorite healthy snack for the child. Give it to the grandparents in private and let them know the child will be thrilled with this treat. Then promise them that you will never give the child this treat at home. It will be something special he gets just from Grandma and Grandpa. You will be providing an alternative to unacceptable practices and will still be helping to forge the friendship between grandparent and grandchild. In this way, you are able to protect your child from detrimental practices or substances without causing a major family conflict. And Grandma will get the credit for giving the child something he loves.

Parents Provide Times for Grandparents and Grandchildren to Be Together

As we provide times for our children and their grandparents to be together, we must be sensitive to the needs of grandparents. Their health may be failing, their hearing going, and their tolerance for confusion lessening. We should be alert to signs that they've had enough. Encourage them to tell a grandchild when they need to rest. Explain to a young child, "Grandpa needs rest and quiet. He can't keep up with you, just like your little brother can't keep up with you. So, if we give him some time alone, then he will feel better again. It isn't that Grandpa doesn't love you. He does. But he is just tired and he can't play anymore."

Our goal is to instill a sense of compassion rather than ridicule or bitterness. Our attitude will be the key as to whether we accomplish our goal.

Much can be gained by making arrangements for your children to visit their grandparents by themselves.

Virginia is the oldest of five children. When she was young, her parents were exhausted with caring for her and four younger siblings. A special treat for Virginia was to spend the night with her grandmother all by herself. Grandmother let Virginia sleep in her big bed with her and listened to her talk. Virginia needed someone with time to listen. When she wasn't chosen as editor of her school paper in junior high, Grandmother comforted her. Whatever was of concern to her was of concern to Grandmother. She had time simply to listen, and she often gave good advice. Today at age 30 with three boys of her own, Virginia still calls her grandmother for advice.

Virginia's wise parents realized Grandmother could do things and say things they could not. They were thrilled with the special friendship that had developed between their child and her grandmother.

As parents, we must take the initiative in building bridges between our children and their grandparents. Our bridges will be either strong and carefully crafted or rickety and ill kept. When we choose to honor our parents, to help them and our children know each other, and to plan time for our children to be with their grandparents by themselves, we are building strong bridges; and even more, we make it possible for our parents and in-laws to experience the joys of grandparenting.

Why Grandparenting Is Special

Grandparenting is a special time in life, and there is no greater gift we can give our parents than the presence of their grandchildren. Why?

It's a Second Chance for Them to Get It Right

One reason being a grandparent is so special is that it's a second chance at parenting. Grandparents have the opportunity to redeem the mistakes they made with their own children.

The Scriptures say, "I will repay you for the years the locusts have eaten" (Joel 2:25). In a sense, God will help us make up for the mistakes we made with our own children by giving us a second chance with our grandchildren.

Our friends Joe and Beth did not come into a deep faith until their children were nearly grown. As they have begun to know God, they have been thrilled with what they are learning. The Scriptures have come alive to them in a way they never understood before. And prayer has become more natural as they've realized they can talk to God about anything.

But the joy they have felt has been tinged with sadness, for they wish they had known of God's personal love when their children were small. How they would love to have shared their faith with them and helped them come to Christ at an early age! But it was not to be, and our friends have discovered a great blessing—grandchildren.

Their three-year-old granddaughter stays with them frequently. Each evening Grandpa reads Bible stories to her and prays with her, telling her about his new friend, Jesus. Grandma takes her on walks and points out everything God has made. This child is being nurtured in the faith, and the grandparents are blessed because they have a new opportunity for sharing the love of Christ with her.

They Finally Have Time to Enjoy Children

Grandparents don't seem to be in such a hurry or have such a great need to be accomplishing tasks as when their children were small. They are better able to enjoy each moment because they realize they don't have that many left. This makes it easier to take special moments with a grandchild instead of worrying about what's not getting done.

They Aren't the Major Disciplinarians

Grandparents finally get to spoil somebody—their grandchildren—just a little! Of course, they must do it in a healthy way and with lots of love.

At Grandma's, children get to stay up late and have two desserts. And she doesn't tell them to wear different clothes or change their hairstyles. It's great for grandparents to spoil a little, if they still support the standards of parents. But they should never undermine the parents' authority. If something is questionable, they should ask the parents' permission before going ahead.

Their Grandchildren Listen to Them

Sixteen-year-old Alice was overweight, and it was affecting her self-image. Her grandmother said to her one day, "I've been wanting to talk to you about something. You are so beautiful and so sweet, but I know you would feel better if you could lose some weight. I know you can do it, and I'll support you in any way that I can."

Their conversation continued for some time, and Alice accepted from her grandmother what she would have resented hearing from her mother.

Grandparents can say things parents never could and get away with it. Being one generation removed helps grandchildren be more open to their advice.

Friendship Becomes Natural When They Play
with Their Grandchildren

If children are comfortable with grandparents, they will come for advice when they are teens. But sometimes the older generation runs out of ideas of ways to play with them. Here's help you can pass along!

To Grandparents: Things to Do with Grandchildren

1. Visit them and have them visit you—by themselves.
2. Every year, write them letters on their birthday. Share your thoughts about life and your prayers and dreams for them. Make this separate from a birthday card. Let it be more like an essay or a legacy you want to leave them. Their parents will save these letters, and when your grandchildren are grown, those letters, bundled with old rubber bands, will be great treasures.

3. If you work, take them to work with you. Introduce them to folks in your office or place of employment.
4. Collect bugs in a jar together.
5. Go fishing.
6. Take them for ice cream cones.
7. Read to them a lot. Don't miss reading together the *Chronicles of Narnia* by C.S. Lewis.
8. Designate a bookshelf in your home that's especially for them.
9. Get some toys (garage sales are a great place) and have a shelf in your house just for them. Try to have toys they don't have at home.
10. Work a puzzle with them.
11. Teach them to play chess or backgammon.
12. Get them a tool box and tools. Teach them how to hammer nails into a board and let them work beside you.
13. Go for a walk. Take a paper bag and let them collect anything that God has made (a rock, a leaf, etc.). Talk about how wonderful God is to have made so many different things for us to enjoy.
14. Learn a verse like Psalm 98:7-9 together.
15. Build castles with a deck of cards. Laugh when they fall down.
16. Tell them stories about their parents when they were little. Tell the funny and naughty things they did. (Parents of young children, now is the time to keep a journal of the funny things your children do and say so that you will remember them for *your* grandchildren!)
17. Shut off all the lights in and around the house and go outside on a clear night. Take a blanket, sit in the yard, and count stars. As you sit there, learn the verse, "The heavens declare the glory of God; the skies proclaim the work of his hands" (Ps. 19:1).
18. Cook s'mores over a fire. (S'mores are graham crackers filled with roasted marshmallows and chocolate bars.)
19. Look at old photos and movies together.
20. Take funny pictures of the kids and help them make a scrapbook to take home.
21. Collect leaves in the fall. Iron them between two pieces of wax paper. Hang them with a string in the window.
22. Pray for them and with them.
23. Pray for their future mates and for the parents who are raising those future mates.
24. Be interested in what they are interested in. Ask good questions. Listen.

25. Walk in the woods near a golf course. Collect lost golf balls. Put them in egg cartons and grade them according to their condition.
26. Play checkers and sometimes let them win.
27. Keep a bag of funny dress-up clothes for play. Take pictures of them in dress-ups. Frame the picture and let them wrap it to give to a parent.
28. Take them on field trips.
29. Take them to the fire station. Call ahead and see if there is a special time for climbing on the truck.
30. Go for a walk on the beach. Let them bury you in the sand.
31. Build drip castles in the sandbox or at the beach. (Mix water and sand and let it drip through your fingers to make beautiful towers for your castle.)
32. Make a fort out of a card table with a blanket thrown over it.
33. Get an empty refrigerator box from an appliance store. Cut windows and doors for a playhouse. Let them decorate it with markers.
34. Frame a picture they draw for you. Hang it in a place of prominence when they come to visit.
35. Collect rocks.
36. Play hide and seek in the house. Let the children hide and take a long time finding them.
37. Play volleyball with balloons.
38. Teach them to cook. Give them an apron, bowl, and ingredients.
39. Go to their athletic events and performances. If you live far away, phone and ask them to tell you all about it.
40. Have a hula-hoop contest.
41. Have cousins visit together without parents.

We wanted to do so many of these things with our own children when they were little, but we just never got to it. That's why being a grandparent is so much fun. If you are a grandparent, enjoy your grandchildren. If you are not a grandparent yet, start a list now of the things you want to do when you become one.

If you haven't had the experience of a close relationship with your own grandparent, you may wonder how to begin being one. Find a couple who have a special relationship with their grandchildren and learn from them. They can be role models for you. Ask if you can join them sometime when they are with their grandchildren and listen, watch, and learn from them.

One of the blessings of the church is that we can go to others to fill out what is lacking in our own experience. Those who are consulted are blessed because they are sharing their wisdom, and you are blessed because you are learning from it. That is how God intended His Body—the Church—to work.

As I ended my visit with Grandma Monie's grandchildren, I asked, "What do you appreciate most about your grandmother?"

One granddaughter replied, "I appreciate the fact that she prays for me. One night I tiptoed in to kiss her good night, and there she was on her knees by the side of the bed, with her wrinkled hands folded and her white head bowed."

I knew what this granddaughter was talking about because I, too, know she prays for me. I, too, have seen her on her knees praying for her children and her grandchildren. You see, Grandma Monie is my mother-in-law.

Focus Questions

Meditate on 2 Timothy 1:1-14.

1. Describe the different relationships you see in this passage. Note especially the generations.
2. Who influenced Timothy's faith? How did they do so?
3. What reminders and instructions did Paul give to his "son" Timothy? Who can you care for in a similar fashion?

Family Friendship Builder

To help children grow in the character trait of thoughtfulness, have a family brainstorming session around the dinner table and see how many ways your family can think of to be kind to grandparents. Then follow through with some of the ideas by letting a family member do one of them each week.

CHAPTER 15

Caring for the Extended Family

And be kind to one another;
tender-hearted, forgiving each other,
just as God in Christ also has forgiven you.

Ephesians 4:32

*I*t was a clear December morning in Colorado. Sun poured though the tall, bare trees and shone down on the remaining snow patches, making them look like a sparkling array of diamonds.

Sally and her three-year-old great-niece Megan were playing chase in the yard when they noticed a beautiful blue crocus peeking through the snow at the base of a tree.

"Megan," Sally exclaimed, "isn't God special to let us see a crocus blooming in December in Colorado?"

"Aunt Sally," the child replied, "God can do anything He wants to, can't He?"

"Yes, He can, sweetheart."

And Sally began to tell Megan about the many things that God can do. It was a precious talk between a great-aunt and a niece.

Sally has had many special times with her niece and nephews and now in turn with their children. It hasn't been easy because she has always lived far away from them. But she has worked at cultivating these extended-family relationships.

Each Christmas, Sally would give her niece and nephews a special ornament. Carefully chosen, the ornament represented a current interest in their lives. The year her great-niece Rachel got her first pair of eyeglasses, her ornament was a tiny pair of glasses! When her nephew played baseball, he received a small baseball mitt inscribed with his name to hang on the tree. The ornaments are stored in their owner's box, and every year when the boxes are opened, the family has a wonderful time remembering past events in each other's lives. Each box becomes a personal diary, telling the story of the child's life. Now this tradition is continuing into the next generation with Sally's eight great-nieces and great-nephews.

Sally phones often and speaks individually with the children. She wants to know about their best friends, their favorite teachers, and what sports they are playing. Vacations are shared with these families, and she always tries to spend time alone with each child. She calls them by special names—names that uplift and affirm. Megan is "Marvelous Megan" and Nate is "Nifty Nate."

As a young, single girl, Sally always assumed she would marry and have children of her own. But as time passed and she remained single, she began to realize that marriage was unlikely. She did not want to become preoccupied with her singleness, because in doing so, she knew she might miss out on many things God had for her. So she chose to concentrate on God's blessings, realizing that her niece and nephews were three of the greatest gifts God had given her.

Sally saw that she had a wonderful opportunity to influence the lives of her extended family. God had given her this specific family. Reflecting on Deuteronomy 6:4-8, she began to pray that she would be close to her niece and nephews and would help them come to love the Lord. God has answered her prayers, and now Sally spends time loving her great-nieces and great-nephews and praying that they, too, will walk in the ways of Christ.

Recently, her nephew Don said, "What's so special about Aunt Sally is that she was always there for me when I was little. She'd come to visit, bringing the latest silly songs, and she'd play them on the piano for us. She'd make us laugh, and I knew she loved being with us. Now my kids have become her kids. She's very involved in their lives. Aunt Sally chose to be involved with us and we have all been blessed by her."

Don't we all wish we had an Aunt Sally? At this moment you may not have one, but you *can* find a special aunt or uncle and you *can* become one yourself. A large extended family is possible for each of us. We need to think of extended family in two categories: our biological extended family (aunts, uncles, nieces, nephews, and cousins), and our spiritual extended family (the family of Christ).

The French have captured this sense in one of their words for family, *la petite église,* which translated means "the little church." We are to treat each other in our families the same way we treat one another in the Body of Christ. We should treat an elderly man in the church with the same compassion that we would give an older uncle in our family and vice versa.

We may not have a large biological extended family, or if we do, we may live far from them. But we should have an extended family of Christ where we live. We need both kinds of extended families.

What are some practical ways in which we can build friendships with our biological extended family? And how do we develop an extended family of people to whom we are not related? Let's explore some ideas.

Building Bridges with Our Biological Extended Family

Choose to Cultivate Extended-Family Relationships

My friend Aunt Sally could have retreated into the world of single friends, but instead she intentionally *chose* to nurture relationships with her family.

She was aware of the sense of family history she shared with her niece and nephews. She knew it was her family who would be there for life's significant events: births, marriages, and deaths. And she had the assurance that God had chosen her to be in *this* family for a reason. She wanted to be a positive influence on the generations to come.

Another friend, Barbara, has a great-aunt who is in her eighties. Auntie recently moved into a retirement community in Barbara's hometown. Although she is a busy young mother with two small children, Barbara has *chosen* to reach out to her great-aunt. On moving day, Barbara helped her unpack. She phones regularly, asking what she can do for her. Her little girls visit Auntie and have even slept over at Auntie's retirement community home all by themselves.

Recently, Barbara asked her great-aunt if she would lead a Bible study for her and some of her friends. Now, every Thursday, Auntie teaches 13 young mothers the Book of Acts. And she encourages them in their job of parenting. Why does Barbara have such a special relationship with her great-aunt? Her own mother holds the key.

Barbara's mother has always cared for Auntie. She has included her in family events, invited her to go places, had luncheons for her and her friends, and introduced her to her own friends. Because Auntie loves chocolate chip cookies, she makes them for her from scratch.

Barbara grew up watching her mother's love for Auntie, and so it was perfectly natural for her to reach out to her great-aunt as well. Now Barbara's little girls are learning how to care by watching their mother. And four generations are being blessed.

An unusual family? Perhaps. But this same warmth and love is possible for anyone. No matter what has gone before you, *you* can be the first in a generation of a family that genuinely loves each other.

You can choose to begin in a new way to love each other, and it will filter down through generations to come. If you are older, seek specifically to care for younger extended-family members. If you are a young family member, intentionally choose to care for and to honor the older members.

Help Your Children Build Relationships with Extended Family

Our niece Sue and our nephew Tucker have lived with us at different times. At 28, Sue is an example of a woman not willing to settle for less than God's best in a relationship with a man. She has been pursued by several different men, but she has not responded except in friendship. She has been determined to wait for God's best for her, whether that means remaining single or being married to a godly husband. And waiting has been hard and lonely at times. Last week, she became engaged to a wonderful man who loves the Lord and who is just right for her. How glad she is that she waited! She has modeled for my 14-year-old twins the value of waiting in relationships with guys and refusing to settle for less than God's best.

Tucker, also in his twenties, has worked in our youth ministry. He has illustrated for my children the sheer joy of life. His life shows that believers have fun—the Christian life is not dull. Tucker speaks the teenagers' language. Our twins can talk about relationships with him and they listen to his advice.

These two cousins have been great role models for my kids, and they have also given my kids a vision for caring about and helping other cousins come to know Christ. Because Tucker and Sue are older, my kids look up to them. Now my children realize they need to reach out to *their* younger cousins the way Sue and Tucker have to them.

Reaching out may not come naturally. We have to remind our children to do it and tell them how. When our son Chris went to visit his grandmother, I specifically reminded him to play with his little cousin.

"Invite him to play ball with you," I suggested. "He looks up to you because you are big. Be his friend now, and in time you may be able to talk with him about his faith."

This gives Chris an understanding that he is important to someone. It builds him up while planting the seeds of his responsibility toward family. Sometimes I remind him of the example of his older cousins, Sue and Tucker, and the roles they have played in his life.

Spend Time Together as Families

For years we went to the beach with my sister and her family, my two brothers and their families, and my parents. A highlight of the week was THE EVENT. Each vacation, one family took the responsibility of planning a special day for the whole crowd.

The year of the International Summer Olympics, we had Family Olympics on the beach. Three-legged races and balloon tosses with all ages caused hysterical laughter. Best of all, everyone got a prize. During the summer of '84 when national politicians were battling each other, we had our own political conventions as two young cousins vied for president with lighthearted humor.

Not only have these extended-family vacations been fun, they have provided opportunities for our children and their cousins to get to know each other. In addition, we adults get to know one another's children as we play and work on projects together.

Our times at the beach have given our children a sense that they are part of something bigger than their own immediate family. They have a larger network of support. And that is a wonderful thing to have today.

We can't spend all of our vacation time with the extended family. Families need some time alone together. And there is not enough time and money to do both. So be with your extended family sometimes, and other times your immediate family. Whether with the extended or immediate family, being away from daily schedules and relaxing together can add yet another layer to family friendships.

Give Your Children Time with Extended Family When You Are Not There

Mimi invited two of her grandsons to visit her all by themselves. One boy was the youngest in his family; his cousin was a middle child. At eight and nine, these two cousins were full of energy. But most amazing was their behavior. It was good! Because there were no siblings to compete with and no parents to give instructions, both boys assumed a maturity they did not usually exhibit. For once the young one wasn't the baby anymore. He felt and acted grown up. For once the middle one didn't always have to be making peace between the youngest and the oldest. They had a wonderful time with each other and with their grandmother.

Two teenage girls, first cousins, went to camp together. Because they lived far apart, they did not know each other well. But since each was the only person the other knew at the camp, they gravitated toward one another and became close. Today, they still look to that experience as a special bonding time in their relationship.

Our daughter Allison tells of a special experience she had visiting her aunt, my sister, Fran. "What was so much fun was that because I was with her by myself, I felt like I became her friend, not just her niece. And I got to know my own mom better through her sister's eyes."

When we make it possible for different family members to be together away from their own parents, we are adding another layer to extended-family friendships.

Be Sensitive to Special Needs

Sometimes a family member will have a special need. It might be the need to be left alone. This happened to my friend Jean, who is single.

For a couple of years, Jean lived with her brother, who was also single and working in the same town. Then her brother got married and Jean moved out. She still had a key to the apartment, however, and because she had left some things in the apartment, she frequently stopped by. But she didn't always feel welcomed by his new wife. After a talk with her brother, Jean realized that, as newlyweds, they needed some space and not a favorite sister popping in at all hours. And so, Jean returned the key and quit visiting. After a year, the new wife began to invite Jean over and a friendship started to develop.

There will always be special needs in our families. We will not be able to be best friends with every person in the family. Nor will we agree with every life-style within the extended family.

We must uphold moral standards in our own homes. A cousin comes to visit, bringing a girlfriend with whom he expects to sleep. You put them in separate rooms. They are not married, and you must keep a high standard for your own children. Take control of what goes on in your house. But while you lay down rules, at the same time do whatever you can to build bridges of friendship with them. Perhaps one day you will be the person to reach a rebellious family member. Keep your door open and your welcome genuine. You can love a person without approving of his life-style.

"But what if my parents don't care about me or my children?" you ask. "What if they have no interest in being grandparents to my kids? What if I am estranged from my extended family?"

Just keep caring and praying for them. Send cards. Phone to say, "I'm thinking about you and just wanted to say hello." Even if there's little response, keep doing it. And encourage your children to develop relationships with estranged family members. Your children will have to understand the tension between you. They may have to be the initiators in the relationship. Your children's overtures may be received when yours are not. And it may be your children who will one day become the bridge to a restored relationship between you and another family member.

Adopt some extended family. If you are lonely because you have no family or because you are estranged from them, reach out and become an "aunt" or "uncle" to someone. You will be blessed and they will be blessed.

The Body of Christ as the Extended Family

When we moved to Virginia, we had five children under the age of eight. Our twins were just six weeks old, and because I was nursing them, I was up a lot at night. I was exhausted. We had no friends or family in the area, and I was lonely. This was the beginning of my special relationship with our neighbor Edith. In her eighties, she soon became extended family to us.

Often our two-year-old son Chris would go to her house in the late afternoon and Edith would read to him. I felt sorry for Chris, a middle child, because I was too exhausted to give him the time he needed. Edith stepped in and filled the gap. And she prayed for me and encouraged me when I felt like the worst mother in the world.

A young couple, Bob and Sandy Smith, moved into a new neighborhood. Working in their garden one day, they met their neighbors Tom and Carol. Several years older than Bob and Sandy, Tom and Carol had never had children of their own. But they fell in love with the Smiths' new baby, Laura. A fondness grew between the two couples, and Bob and Sandy asked Tom and Carol to become Laura's godparents.

Tom and Carol hadn't been in a church for years. It just wasn't important to them, but they knew it was to the Smiths. Many times the Smiths had asked them to go to church, but they always seemed to have an excuse. Now, however, as godparents to little Laura, they wanted to set an example for her, so they agreed to go to church with the Smiths. There they found love and warmth and a clear presentation of the Good News of Christ. And they recognized the emptiness in their lives. Within a few weeks, both Carol and Tom became followers of Christ. Their faith began to grow as they got involved in the life of the church, and their friendship with the Smiths grew even deeper.

Adjoining backyards and a common love of a child were instruments in filling a spiritual gap in the lives of two people. Now this nonbiological extended family is reaching out to other families in their neighborhood.

A couple in our church took an interest in a single mother and her teenage son. They began inviting them over regularly for dinner. The man expressed an interest in her son and became for him a positive older male friend. When the boy had tough decisions to make, he went to his male friend for advice. The friend listened and encouraged him. He prayed for him. This two-parent family offered support to a single parent. Because she was raising her son alone, she needed other adults with whom to discuss parenting issues. From her, the two-parent family learned how to care for those from broken homes. Now their daughter is especially sensitive to children in single-parent families and often takes the initiative for reaching out to those who are in her school. From one family, guidance was received; from the other, sensitivity was learned. Both were blessed as they filled the gaps in each other's family.

Our friends Bob and Elaine have lost all four of their parents. They were very close to them and miss them terribly. One of the hardest things about the loss is that Bob and Elaine miss telling about their children's accomplishments. You can always brag to grandparents. It can be awkward to brag to your peers.

Elaine's older friend Marji has begun to fill a gap left by the death of these grandparents. Now when her kids receive an award, Elaine calls Marji to share her news. A grandmother herself, Marji understands the joy it gives Elaine to share her children's accomplishments.

Filling in the gaps is one of the ways the family of Christ works. The Scriptures say, "We will in all things grow up into him who is the head, that is Christ. From him the whole body, joined and held together by every supporting ligament, grows and builds itself up in love, as each part does its work" (Eph. 4:15, 16).

We cannot grow alone. We are all interconnected, and we need one another. We grow only as each part does its work. The extended family of believers makes up the Body. We may be related by blood or we may be related by adoption, but we need people who can fill in the gaps for us. And we need to be willing to fill in the gaps for someone else.

Jesus Himself needed the extended family of believers to fill in a gap for Him. As He hung on the cross in agony, knowing His death was close, He looked out into the crowd and saw His beloved mother. His pain in seeing her pain must have been overwhelming. With a broken heart and eyes filled with tears, He gazed tenderly at her. And then He saw the disciple whom He loved standing nearby.

Jesus said to His mother, "'Dear woman, here is your son,' and to the disciple, 'Here is your mother.' From that time on, this disciple took her into his home" (John 19:26, 27).

John, Jesus' beloved disciple, became a son in Mary's extended family. He filled the gap that Jesus left when He died.

Yes, God created us to live in a family. And it is good.

Focus Questions

Meditate on Ephesians 4.

1. What traits described here do you want to characterize your extended family?
2. What is your responsibility to the rest of your family?
3. What are some behaviors you need to put away? Is there an action you need to take in a relationship?

Family Friendship Builder

What do I need to do to build bridges with my extended family? Is there someone I should write today?

Do I need to be available to become an "aunt" or a "grandparent" for someone? Who might that be? Should our family adopt a single parent and her (or his) children to be our extended family?

Plan a family dinner for sometime next month and invite someone you feel God may want you to reach out to as a part of your extended family.

CHAPTER 16

Friendships in Single-Parent and Blended Families

For the Lord your God is God of gods and Lord of lords,
the great God, mighty and awesome,
who shows no partiality and accepts no bribes.
He defends the cause of the fatherless and the widow,
and loves the alien, giving him food and clothing.
Deuteronomy 10:17, 18

It could have been anywhere in the country. A shady street lined with trees whose branches reach over the sidewalks and form a canopy. Five homes spread out along this street. They are each as different as are the families that live inside. One yard is carefully manicured, while another is ill kept. One home is noisy with lots of coming and going, whereas weeks go by without anyone visiting the home next door. Both sadness and joy are experienced in every one of these five homes.

But the homes in this neighborhood have one thing in common: They have all been touched by divorce, and now they are each trying to build families marked by love for one another. Let's see what we can learn from them.

Married with a Stepchild

Jeff and Ann and their son, Tom, live on the corner. Actually, Tom is Ann's son by her first marriage. He was just four when she married for the second time. Becoming a husband and a parent at the same time was a challenge for stepfather Jeff. One of the most frustrating things was that Tom's real dad, who had deserted the family, would pop in intermittently and act like everything was just great. Often when he appeared, he would take little Tom out and buy him a gift. One particular day after being out with his "real" dad, Tom announced to Jeff, "My daddy bought me a big truck. What are *you* going to do?" The child was unconsciously setting up a competition between his biological dad and the dad who lived with him. This feeling that he couldn't compete was just one of the challenges facing Jeff as he struggled to build a friendship with his young stepson.

And then there were the questions the young boy asked: "Why did my other daddy leave? Why can't he live here, too?" Difficult questions to answer.

In the process of building a friendship with the boy, Jeff has gained some valuable wisdom and learned several practical tips that will help others in a similar situation.

- Refuse to compete with the "real" dad or mom. When his biological dad buys Tom a gift, Jeff responds, "That's swell." Period. And he refuses to get drawn into any type of competition. You are not trying to one-up the other parent. You are trying to build a sound friendship with the child.
- Be positive about the child's biological dad. Don't bad-mouth him. Don't dwell on him in conversations. Don't allow the child to become caught in the middle of a popularity contest between parents. The most important thing is the child.
- Answer questions briefly and truthfully. When little Tom asked his mother, "Why did my other dad leave?" she replied, "He didn't want to live with us anymore."

  As he grows up, he will want more explanation, but he is not asking for it now. Too often we feel we must explain everything, giving more information than children want or need at a particular time.
- Make a conscious choice to make a difference in the child's life. Jeff determined from the beginning that Tom would be his son. "We're getting married, all three of us," was how little Tom described the

wedding. Jeff's commitment to Tom was as strong as his commitment to Ann. It wasn't halfway. And this has made their marriage even stronger.

- Spend time with the child. As in all families, time together is crucial for building a friendship. Pick something the child likes to do and do it regularly—just the two of you. Develop little habits like praying together at bedtime. Reassure the child that you will never leave as the "real" father did.

- Teach the child. Realize you have a wonderful opportunity to teach this child, to impact his or her life. Make a list of things you want to teach the child. This gives you a vision and helps you become an initiator, not merely a responder. And it's more positive to initiate learning than to merely fall into the trap of reacting to a child's stages of growth.

  Jeff's list of things he wants to teach Tom include the value of hard work (he taught Tom how to mow the yard), how to live by the golden rule (to treat others as you want to be treated), and to view every person as someone you can learn from (Jeff introduces Tom to all kinds of people).

- You are the boss, the child is not. You are the parent. Don't be too lax in discipline or withhold affection because you are not the "real" parent. If you are living with a child, you are now the real parent. It may take time for your role as disciplinarian to emerge. Be patient and generous with affection.

Sitting behind Jeff, Ann, and Tom in church, I watched as Tom, now nine, snuggled up to Jeff and put his head on his shoulder. As Jeff's arm reached around him and gave him an affectionate squeeze, I silently marveled, *Thank You, God, for giving these two to each other.*

An Older Child of Divorce

Across the street live Amy, her mother, and a younger brother. She recently finished college and now has her first professional job. At 22, she is constantly on the go, and her car is either pulling in or out of the drive-way. Amy's dad and mom were divorced when she was only five. Even though she was small when her dad left, it has been a painful process for Amy. Her parents fought many legal battles in a messy divorce.

Her father remarried and she found herself with instant stepbrothers. She and her younger brother began to spend every other weekend with her dad and his new family. She had difficulty adjusting to the different rules of her two homes. At her mom's house, it was all right to eat sugar, but other junk food wasn't allowed. But when she went to her dad's, sugar was not allowed, but junk food was fine. She struggled to keep the different expectations straight.

She also struggled with trying to balance the amount of time she spent with each parent. Amy often felt guilty because she spent more time with one parent than the other. And then there were those awkward family events that both parents attended. Whom should she sit next to? To whom should she talk?

Hardest of all was the feeling of being caught in the middle when her parents fought. She didn't like it when her mother told her she needed to make her dad pay a bill. She respected her mom and she loved both parents, but sometimes she felt trapped between them.

Even though Amy has had a difficult time growing up, she has gained wisdom far beyond her years. I asked her what advice she would give divorced parents that would help foster family friendships. Here is her list:

- Don't fight through your children or put them in the middle when loyalty dilemmas arise. Children need to be free to establish their own relationships with each parent. Parents must discuss their problems or lawyers need to handle them. Don't make your children the messengers.
- Lay the groundwork for friendships in a second marriage. Spend time with the children involved before the wedding, so they can begin to build friendships with the new spouse and, if there are children from both previous marriages, with each other. After the wedding, take vacations together. Doing special things together will enable the stepbrothers and stepsisters to have shared experiences that will begin to give them a history together.
- Treat the children equally. When it's your weekend to have the kids from both families and you go shopping, give each child the same amount of spending money. It's awkward for the stepchildren when they're not given any spending money.
- Noncustodial parents have to work doubly hard. If you do not have primary custody of the children, make an extra effort to spend consistent time with them. Beginning friendships in the teen years is hard if you haven't been there as the children were growing up.
- Pray for your children and nurture their faith. Let them see that you are depending on God to meet your needs and theirs.

As I visited with Amy, I was amazed at her maturity. But most of all, I was touched by her lack of resentment, by her love for both her parents, and by the vital faith she has. It's her faith in a loving, forgiving God that makes the difference.

A Single Parent with Two Children

Next door to Amy's house is Nancy's home. Her grass needs trimming and the paint on the windowsills is peeling, but there are happy noises coming from the family dinner table.

Nancy's life is a busy one of juggling a full-time, demanding job and raising two children by herself. She never expected her life to be like this. When her son was three and she was pregnant with her second child, her husband left her for someone else. She was stunned. A sense of failure, anger, and deep exhaustion overwhelmed her. And all of a sudden she had to do it all. When the car broke down, when the plumbing backed up, when the kids got sick, she had to take care of things alone. The details of merely getting through the day seemed impossible. And then, as the children began to grow, discipline became a challenge. No one could back her up and say, "You must not talk to your mother like that."

She had to do it all herself, and it was very hard. But along the way she, too, has learned some valuable lessons that will encourage you as you seek to cultivate friendships in a difficult family situation.

- Relinquish bitterness. Sound easy? It's not. It's probably the hardest thing you will have to do, and it's not something you do once and it's finished. Rather, letting go of bitterness is a long road in which, mile by mile, you give it up one piece at a time. Sometimes you may not even realize that you are bitter. This happened to Nancy. A friend said to her, "You must get rid of this bitterness or you will have an unhappy life."

  Nancy listened to her friend. She realized that she needed to be honest with herself about her part in the failed marriage. She began to look at her former partner with pity instead of anger. And she got some professional help.

- Seek good counseling. Talking to a professional counselor can be helpful. Be sure you get references on the counselor. The counseling should be biblically based. But do not automatically assume because someone is a Christian counselor, he is a good counselor. He may be very bad. So seek recommendations from someone you trust.

- Pursue fellowship. Nancy finds her greatest support comes from meeting with other couples. She initiates family get-togethers. Often on Sundays, she invites another family home from church for lunch. It is brief, casual, and a wonderful means of exposing her children to two-parent families. In addition, these couples provide a sounding board for her to discuss her challenges as a single parent.

    Meeting with other single parents in a support group can also be beneficial. But you need to ask the question, "Is this particular group helping me in a positive way or causing me to nurse my bitterness?" If the group is dragging you down, it is best to stop meeting with them.
- Agree with your former mate not to argue in front of the children. Perhaps he's late bringing them home on a school night. Welcome the children and then walk him to the car for a private discussion or talk later by phone. It is not the children's problem. It's yours. So work it out as best you can and leave the kids out of it.
- Be firm with the discipline. Even though you have no backup and you feel alone, still be firm. You are building for the future. Seek the advice and support of other couples with children. Ask them to talk to your children if that would be helpful. If you have been having two-parent families over, they will already have a relationship with your children. Keep in close contact with your extended family. This will give your children a sense of rootedness and security.

Nancy's life is a challenge, but she no longer radiates bitterness. Instead she is encouraging and upbeat, and she is more firmly convinced that God is able to bring good out of any situation.

A Blended Family with Seven Children

As you walk up the street, Mike and Sharon's home stands out. Toys are scattered about the yard, and several bikes and a pair of roller blades lie in a pile by the front door. Two children dash around the corner of the house, chasing after a ball, while another rushes out the front door to a friend's house. It's all the normal chaos of a home with seven kids.

This family hasn't always been together. Mike's first wife left him with four young girls to raise. Sharon had three sons by previous marriages. She had been a single parent for several years and had been striving to bring stability into her life. Mike and Sharon met in church and became friends. Their two families spent a lot of time together. When they married, their children already knew each other. This was helpful, but they've still faced many challenges. Blending two families with seven children ages seven to 15 has not been easy.

There's a big gap in the life of this family. The two families have no common early history together, so there are many things they don't know about one another—things that explain certain behaviors. And the patterns of discipline have been different. Everything is new and expectations are often disappointed. The tendency exists to attribute any crisis between the children to the fact that this is a blended family. It's easy to forget that many families with several children are experiencing the same tensions.

Sharon and Mike have learned some helpful lessons as they've struggled to build a family marked by love rather than dissension.

- Don't ever use the words "yours" or "mine" when discussing the children. They are *ours*.
- Agree to have a time of venting feelings with your spouse. Their seven-year-old daughter was driving her mother crazy, and Sharon felt like she wanted to lock her in the closet for a few years. She needed Mike to simply listen to her feelings and not offer advice or counsel. Instead he said, "I know how you must be feeling. You feel like you're going nuts."

   After Sharon vented her feelings, she and Mike set up a time to meet later to discuss the situation and make some decisions. The next time it will likely be Mike who needs Sharon to listen.
- Discuss and agree on a discipline policy with your spouse. Listen to one another's observations. Go over your discipline policy at a planned family meeting so everyone hears it. Then when a child says, "I never heard that," you can remind him that he was in the family meeting where it was discussed. This is helpful in all families with numerous children. It can be easy for a parent to forget who they told what. So do it when everyone is present.
- To cultivate friendships between the children, give them time together in pairs. Even a disgusting chore can have its purpose, because it gives the two who are working together a chance to complain about *Mom* instead of complaining about each other! All the principles for turning sibling rivalry into friendship found in chapter 10 apply to blended families in the same way they do to other families.

- Help the children reach out to the missing parent. Remember Mom's birthday. Remember Dad on Father's Day and other special days. No matter what the missing partner has done or not done, she or he is still your child's biological parent. Your children should give the missing parent a gift, not because she or he deserves it, but because your children must learn to care. And they may one day be used by God to bring healing.
- Plan family meetings. The first year of their marriage, Mike and Sharon had half-hour meetings with the family several times during the week. They sang together and Mike gave a brief devotional. Often they spent time sharing with each other something they appreciated about another person. As time passed, they discussed whatever needed to be discussed. And it became a practice that if anyone in the family had something to discuss, she or he could ask Dad to call a family meeting.

Raising a blended family is challenging, but it is also filled with blessings—blessings of small, positive steps in a difficult relationship. While Sharon was driving the car the other day, her seven-year-old daughter turned to her and said, "Can I tell you something, Mom? I think you love me the way God loves me."

"Why is that, honey?"

"Well, I do lots of bad things to you because I want my real mom to come home, but you still love me. And you forgive me. I think that's how God loves me."

An Adult Child of Divorce Now Happily Married with Children

Next door to the blended family is a neatly landscaped home. Carefully manicured boxwoods line the front walk, and in the spring, the yard is bright with pansies. Late in the day you might see Joe pulling a rare weed or replanting a fragile flower. Both Sarah and Joe are hard workers. They have carefully and intentionally worked on their yard and on their family life as well.

Sarah grew up in a broken home. She was 14 when her parents divorced. As the oldest child, she became her mother's confidante and emotional support. It was tough on this teen when she was thrust into a role for which she was unprepared. In addition, years of poor communication between her parents did not provide Sarah with a model for good communication in marriage. It was natural for her to come into her own marriage with wounds and fears. Could she and Joe have a successful family?

Fifteen years have passed, and they are now the parents of two teenagers. Their marriage is strong, and their relationship with their children is a model for many young families. They have worked hard at marriage and parenting, and in the process, they've learned some helpful things.

- Put your marriage before your children. Even though Sarah's parents divorced, her mother taught her that God hates divorce. She knew first-hand the pain divorce causes, and she told her children that they should view marriage as a lifelong commitment. To do so, they would need to put their marriages before everything but their relationships with God. It's all too easy to focus on the children first.

  Sarah and Joe have learned to put each other first. If one of the children wants Joe's help, but he is busy doing a project for Sarah, he simply says, "I'm sorry, but I'm helping Mom right now. I will come when I finish."

  The couple's bedroom is a sanctuary. The children have never slept with their parents. Joe and Sarah have maintained a good physical relationship.

  The kids in this family are secure in their parents' marriage, and they are learning skills that will one day help them build good marriages for themselves.

- Develop good communication skills. This is tough, especially if you grew up in a home in which communication was lacking. But you can do it! Talk to other couples who have strong communication skills. Ask them how they do it. Seek good counseling. Read books on marriage and family life. *The Marriage Builder*[1] by Larry Crabb is excellent. When you feel stuck in your career, you do research to find a solution to your problem, and if necessary, you take classes to learn something different or to upgrade your skills. Why wouldn't you give the same time and energy to the most important part of your life—your family? When the tough times come, dig in.

  When things got hard for Sarah, she tended to get depressed, to want to run away, to feel like quitting. But she didn't do any of those things. Why? She remembered the teaching of her mother. Marriage is for keeps. Instead, she put herself in God's hands and relied on His help

through the tough times. She refused to give in to the temptation to quit.
- Talk to your kids about your own experiences and be available to their friends. Sarah has shared much of her background with her children. She wants them to be sensitive to their friends whose parents are divorcing. And she is available to befriend children in pain. Her home has become a sanctuary for young people from broken homes. Sarah and her home have become a light of hope that one day these young people, too, can have a happy family life.

A New Home

At the end of the street, a huge cement mixer's engines whir away. Lumber is piled in neat rows, waiting to be used. Construction workers with hard hats scurry around like bees. Children run up and down the street to see what's happening on the new house.

Just a few weeks ago, this lot was bare. Rocks had to be dug up and trees removed. But now, outlines of a new home are beginning to emerge. It's exciting for this neighborhood. Of course, there will be mistakes made in the building process. The house won't be perfect. There will be things the owners wish they had done differently. But the home will be fresh. Something wonderful is being created from scratch.

Your home may feel barren. There may be many hard places and much pain in your past—but there is hope. No matter what you experienced, you can be the first of a new generation of healthy families. You can break the chain of broken families. Your children and grandchildren can raise families whose members truly love one another.

Paul says in 2 Corinthians 5:17-18, "Therefore if anyone is in Christ, he is a new creation; the old has gone; the new has come. All this is from God, who reconciled us to himself through Christ and gave us the ministry of reconciliation."

A fresh start. A clean slate. A promise of hope. A family whose members are friends with each other. It can all be yours. "For nothing is impossible with God" (Luke 1:37).

Focus Questions

Meditate on 2 Corinthians 5:14-21.

1. What is the ministry of reconciliation that God has given you?
2. What do you need to do for your family to be reconciled?

3. How can you be an encouragement to others who are struggling with building friendships in a damaged family?

Family Friendship Builder

Sharing histories helps us to know each other better, especially if there have been gaps. Set aside a day as Family History Day. This should be a fun event for every family. Let several family members tell about their childhoods. What are their earliest memories? What were their favorite toys when they were children? Who were the adults they especially liked and why? What were the funniest things that happened to them? Look at old photo albums.

Yours Can Be a Family of Friends

James's early memories were a blur of feeling "unsafe and unloved." One terrifying memory was of walking into the kitchen and finding his mother lying in a pool of her own blood. She had tried to kill herself.

His mother, a troubled woman, was in and out of mental hospitals most of his young life. Because of her mental condition, and the fact that his father was away in the military, James and his younger sister were sent to live with grandparents. Soon afterward, his parents divorced.

Several years after the divorce, both his parents remarried. He and his sister returned to live with his father and stepmother. When he was about 12 years old, he learned that his mother had had a new baby girl. Now more than ever, he longed to see her and his half sister. But before he could, his mother committed suicide. Her new husband left town, and no one in the family could find out what had happened to baby Ellie.

For years James wondered where she was. He prayed for and thought about the little sister he did not know. Was she safe? Did someone love her? Where was she?

James grew up, married, and had two children. He had a difficult time working through the pain of his childhood, especially coping with all the unresolved issues—particularly the issue of what had happened to his baby sister. He wondered, *Where is God? Does God care about me, about Ellie? Why did God let this happen?*

As time went on, a friend reached out and invited James and his wife, Mary, to a church where they soon came to know about a personal God who *did* care and who *was* at work in their lives. For the first time in their lives, James and Mary began to find answers to some of life's toughest questions. They both committed their lives to Christ and began to grow in their faith.

James never forgot Ellie. He continued to pray for her. Now he prayed that she, too, would know Christ and His love. He prayed and prayed, but because 28 years had passed, he had little hope of ever finding her. After all, she might be in jail or dead. Even if she were alive, she might not want to know about a half brother.

Then one evening, the phone rang in James's house. It was Ellie. She began to tell her story, and as it unfolded, James wept. Shortly after their mother died, her father gave her to neighbors in the trailer park where they lived. Then he left town. Her adoptive parents changed her name. When she was 12, they told her she had been adopted and that she was an only child. She had no other family. They told her that her birth parents were both dead.

Life was not easy for Ellie. Her adoptive parents were alcoholics and became abusive. At the age of 16, Ellie and an older stepbrother ran away from home. They settled in another state and she went back to high school. About this time, she learned about the love of Christ and committed her life to Him. After graduating from high school, she married and settled down to raise a family.

Soon she received word that her adoptive parents were ill and near death. Although they had caused her much pain, Ellie felt that because Christ had forgiven her sins and given her a new life, she must forgive them. But even harder was a decision to return home to nurse them.

She went, hoping they would tell her something about her past. Who was her birth mother? Her father? Were there any other family members? But still they refused to talk, and when they died, Ellie felt that her prayer to discover her past would remain unanswered.

Wearily, she began sorting through the papers in her parents' desk. In a drawer at the bottom of a pile of papers she discovered her birth mother's death certificate. There in black and white, for the first time in her life, she saw the name of her mother and the date and location of her death. The archives of the local library provided a copy of the obituary.

Finally, at age 28, she discovered that she had a brother, a sister, and a large extended family. She was not alone on earth! Now that she knew her mother's name and where her family had lived, she was able to track down an uncle who told her about James and gave her his phone number. It took her a couple of days to get up her nerve to call James because she didn't know if he would even want to acknowledge her existence.

When James picked up the phone that hot summer evening, first he was stunned, then he began to cry. Tears choked his voice as he began to talk to Ellie for the first time ever. He cried tears of joy for a sister who had been lost and was now found. He cried tears of hope for a family that was fractured and was now beginning to be healed. He cried tears of gratefulness to God, who had protected a runaway teenager, Ellie, and an emotionally wounded young man, himself, and who had revealed Himself to each of them as they sought Him.

God had not forgotten the prayers of a young boy for a sister who was lost. God had been at work all along, even though many times it didn't seem that He was. God had not deserted an abused, lonely little girl. God had not deserted a troubled young man. God had been there for James and Ellie, and He is there for you and me.

So, how do we begin to build a family of friends? We begin with an assurance that God is at work in the lives of our families even when we can't see anything happening; we begin with a commitment to a powerful, loving God who is able to help us; and we begin with a vision of what God intends families to be.

Just as Jenny Butchart had a vision for turning an ugly quarry into a beautiful garden, we can have a *vision* of building a family whose members truly love each other. We may have a good, solid foundation to start with, or we may have only ugliness, like James and Ellie had. Yet, no matter what our backgrounds, we must have a vision. Strong families don't just happen. They take work. Ask God to give you a vision for the kind of family He desires you to have.

We also need *commitment* to a powerful, living God. Only He has the power to forgive, to change lives, to do the impossible. As the psalmist says, "Unless the Lord builds the house, its builders labor in vain" (Ps. 127:1). We cannot build the families we want by ourselves. All of us will fail. We desperately need His forgiveness and His power to keep going. We must give ourselves to Him completely. He has promised that if we ask Him into our hearts, He will come in and will never leave us (see Rev. 3:20; Heb. 13:5). He will forgive us all of our sins and give us His supernatural power (1 John 1:9; Acts 1:8). When we get discouraged, He will pick us up (Ps. 13).

And finally, we need *assurance*. We can have confidence that He is at work in our families even when we can't see it. James certainly couldn't see anything happening. But now he knows that God was always at work, and now he has the assurance that God does not forget His children. We need assurance, too—assurance that God will never leave us.

James and Ellie's God has His hand on you and me and on each of our family members at this very moment. Perhaps you can't see it right now. Maybe you feel like a failure or have deep wounds in your life. Family members may have let you down, or perhaps you have disappointed *them*. Or perhaps things may seem all right just now, but when you consider the future, you are afraid.

No matter where we are in our lives or where we have been, we can have the assurance that our almighty God has His hand on our lives and the lives of our family members. He *is* at work right now. He *will* redeem the past and give us a hope for the future as we look to Him. For our family is really His family.

> *Dear God,*
>
> *How grateful I am that Your power is so strong. Strong enough to raise a man from the dead, to create mountains and seas, to put up kings and bring down governments. And yet Your love is so gentle. Gentle enough to number the hairs on my head, to understand my thoughts, to forgive my sins. I pray, O Lord, that You would be at work in my family, building friendships among its many members. I pray for the generations to come, that they, too, would grow in love for each other. Thank You that You love my family even more than I do and that You are at work in each of us. Thank You that Your hand is on our families, holding them close to Your heart.*
>
> *Amen*

Notes

chapter 7

1. Oswald Chambers, *My Utmost for His Highest* (NIV Edition) (Westwood, N.J.: Barbour and Co., 1988), p. 176.
2. Susan Alexander Yates, *And Then I Had Kids: Encouragement for Mothers of Young Children* (Dallas: Word, 1988), pp. 171, 172.
3. Ibid., p. 173.

chapter 13

1. National Association of Elder Law Attorneys, 1604 North Country Club Road, Tucson, AZ 85716.
2. Worksheet information is from Elaine Metcalf, "Senior Focus," Third Presbyterian Church, 600 Forest Avenue, Richmond, VA 23229.

chapter 16

1. Larry Crabb, *The Marriage Builder: A Blueprint for Couples and Counselors* (Grand Rapids, Mich.: Zondervan, 1982, 1992).

Focus on the Family Publications

Focus on the Family

This complimentary magazine provides inspiring stories, thought-provoking articles, and helpful information for families interested in traditional, biblical values. Each issue also includes a "Focus on the Family" radio broadcast schedule.

Parental Guidance

Close-ups and commentaries on the latest music, movies, television, and advertisements directed toward young people. Parents, as well as youth leaders, teachers, and pastors, will benefit from this indispensable newsletter.

Single-Parent Family

Our newest periodical offers support and encouragement for single parents trying to maintain healthy, stable, and godly homes for themselves and their children.

All magazines are published monthly except where
otherwise noted. For more information regarding these and
other resources, please call Focus on the Family at (719) 531-5181,
or write us at Focus on the Family,
Colorado Springs, CO 80995.